AF346312

The Synfluence

The Synfluence

Becoming Amongst Who We Are

FOUAD KANNEH

Copyright © 2025 Fouad Kanneh

ISBN: 978-3-20984-884-0

DEDICATION

To the dreamers, the doers, and the daring souls who strive
to make the world a better place.
To those who lead with open hearts, unshaken by the storms
of fear and doubt.
To the ones who have faced brokenness but still chose to
rise, rebuild, and inspire others to do the same.
To my family, whose unwavering support has been my
anchor; to my mentors, whose wisdom has been my guide;
and to my colleagues and friends, who remind me every day
what true leadership looks like.
And finally, to you, the reader—may this book ignite a spark
within you, encouraging you to embrace the leader you were
always meant to be.
This is for the journey you've already taken and the one that
lies ahead. Lead boldly.

Table of Contents

ACKNOWLEDGMENTS

A special thank you to the countless individuals whose stories have shaped the narrative of this book. From the leaders I've had the privilege to work with to the ones I've observed from afar, your experiences and insights have been invaluable in creating a book that reflects the complexity and humanity of leadership.

To the team that helped bring this book to life—editors, proofreaders, designers, and everyone behind the scenes—thank you for your tireless efforts and unwavering dedication. Your expertise has transformed an idea into a tangible piece of work I am proud to share with the world.

And lastly, to you, the reader. This book is for you—for the leader you are, the leader you aspire to be, and the journey you are on. Thank you for taking the time to read, reflect, and grow alongside these pages. My hope is that this book inspires you to lead with courage, authenticity, and purpose.

With deep gratitude,
Fouad

ABSTRACT

Leadership is often romanticized as a transformative journey, a magical process that molds individuals into stronger, wiser, and more inspiring versions of themselves. The world is awash with leadership books, TED Talks, and seminars that promise to equip you with the right tools to lead effectively. They preach discipline, resilience, emotional intelligence, and strategic thinking as if these traits can be neatly packaged into a set of instructions that anyone can follow. But here's the brutal truth: leadership doesn't change you. Instead, it ruthlessly reveals who you already are.

Leadership is not a mask you put on; it is a mirror you cannot avoid. It forces you to confront your fears, flaws, motivations, and long-buried emotions. It shines a glaring light on your strengths but also mercilessly exposes your weaknesses. Many individuals ascend into leadership roles expecting to become something different—better, stronger, more capable. Yet, the reality is that leadership does not create a new person; it merely amplifies what already exists within. This book, Synfluence: Becoming Amongst Who We Are, delves into the deep-seated origins of leadership behaviors, demonstrating how much of what defines a leader's style can be traced back to their formative years—childhood experiences, family dynamics, and societal influences.

The Meaning Behind Synfluence

The term Synfluence is a word I created by combining Synchronize and Influence. Synchronize means to cause events to occur at the same time or to align with one another. Influence refers to the capacity to have an effect on character, development, or behavior. In this book, I argue that a leader's formative years act as the synchronizing force that impacts their capacity and behavior as a leader. Their upbringing, whether shaped by chaos, pain, neglect, or nurture, sets the foundation for how they will lead, react, and interact with others. Leadership is not a detached, abstract skillset—it is an extension of personal history and individual experience.

The Roots of Leadership Behavior

The childhood and early experiences of a person are the unseen architects of their leadership style. Whether shaped by a chaotic upbringing, prolonged emotional pain, or neglect, these experiences unconsciously dictate how leaders interact with the world.

Chaos Breeds Chaos: Individuals who grow up in unstable and unpredictable environments may unknowingly replicate that same turbulence in their leadership style. They may be prone to reactive decision-making, thrive in crisis situations, or even create disorder as a subconscious comfort zone.

Pain Breeds Empathy: Those who have suffered and experienced chronic pain often develop heightened empathy, making them more compassionate and understanding leaders. They are attuned to the struggles of others because they have personally endured hardship, which shapes their ability to connect deeply with their team.

Neglect Breeds Insecurity: Leaders who have experienced neglect, dismissal, or a lack of recognition in the past often carry unresolved emotional baggage into their leadership roles. This can manifest as a constant need for validation, an aversion to delegation, or an overly controlling nature.

Recognizing these patterns is the first step toward self-awareness and growth. Without acknowledging the personal histories that shape their behaviors, leaders run the risk of allowing their past to dictate their present and future. This is the fundamental philosophy behind Synfluence—that leadership is not about acquiring a new identity but about understanding and refining the identity that already exists.

Why This Book Matters

The leadership industry often focuses on techniques, strategies, and frameworks—how to be decisive, how to inspire, how to delegate. But few resources dig into the fundamental question: Why do leaders lead the way they do? This book is not about giving you another set of rules to follow. Instead, it is an invitation to look inward and explore how your past shapes your leadership style.

In Synfluence, I will take you on a journey through psychological insights, real-world leadership examples, and personal reflections to help you uncover the hidden forces driving your leadership behavior. You will see that your leadership journey started long before you ever held a title. It began in the moments that shaped you, in the experiences that defined your understanding of power, authority, and responsibility.

This book is not just for CEOs, executives, or managers. It is for anyone who influences others—whether in a professional setting, within a family, or in a community. Because at its core, leadership is not a title; it is a way of being.

The Journey Ahead

In the chapters that follow, we will explore the different facets of leadership identity:

- The Mirror Effect: How leadership reflects personal history rather than reshapes it.
- The Shadows of the Past: Unpacking the unresolved emotional triggers that manifest in leadership decisions.
- The Influence of Pain and Resilience: How hardship creates emotionally intelligent and empathetic leaders.
- Breaking the Cycle: Recognizing and changing self-destructive leadership behaviors.
- The Power of Self-Awareness: Using introspection as a tool for more effective leadership.

By the end of this book, my goal is not to teach you how to become a leader in the traditional sense. Instead, I want to help you understand who you already are as a leader. Because once you recognize and embrace the forces that have shaped you, only then can you lead with true authenticity, clarity, and impact.

Synfluence is not about change—it is about revelation. It is about synchronizing with your past and using that influence to become the leader you were always meant to be.

CHAPTER 1

LEADERSHIP: THE MIRROR YOU CAN'T AVOID

Introduction: Why leadership doesn't change you but exposes you.

You probably don't recognize this name, but Kyla Sanders is one of the most prominent leaders in the world of advocacy in West Africa. Growing up, Kyla faced an uphill battle. Her childhood was a harrowing journey filled with domestic violence and abuse. Her early years were shaped by pain and instability, as she was introduced to sex by an elder cousin at an age when innocence should have been her only companion. Her mother was absent for most of her childhood, serving a lengthy jail term, leaving Kyla to navigate life's harsh realities alone. As she transitioned into adulthood, the trauma followed her, manifesting in a series of violent relationships. These experiences led her down a path of smoking marijuana, deciding to take up work as a stripper, juggling multiple jobs to avoid returning to a volatile home, and even carrying a licensed weapon for protection.

When I first met Kyla, it was her first day as a supervisor. She was known for being hard-headed, a person who refused to listen to others' opinions. For Kyla, leadership was synonymous with dominance and authority. Communication with her was nearly impossible—she would shut people down before they could get a word in. Her subordinates found her intimidating and unapproachable, and even I hesitated to engage with her. Despite her apparent confidence, Kyla's demeanor made her isolated in a role where connection and collaboration were crucial.

A few years later, circumstances changed for both of us. We were promoted to managerial roles simultaneously, and this time, collaboration wasn't optional. Our roles demanded that we communicate frequently—sometimes as often as every twenty minutes. On my first day in this new role, I remember feeling a deep sense of apprehension. How was I going to work with someone who seemed so closed off and resistant to input?

To my surprise, something shifted when we began working together. We developed an unexpected rhythm and understanding. One day, during a short breakroom conversation, Kyla opened up to me. She shared her story—the pain of her past, the struggles she had endured, and the person she had become because of them. In that moment, I saw Kyla not as the intimidating figure I had once feared but as a deeply loving, intelligent, passionate, and emotional human being. The tough exterior she projected was not who she truly was. It was a shield—a deliberate defense mechanism to hide the emotional scars she carried. Kyla's hard-headedness and authoritative style were not born of arrogance but of survival. She feared that allowing people to see her vulnerability would expose her fragility.

The moment I understood this, everything changed. Kyla was no longer the person I struggled to communicate with; she became someone I respected and cared for deeply. Her vulnerabilities gave context to her actions, and her story inspired a desire to support her growth. Over time, I encouraged Kyla to rethink her approach to decision-making. I advised her to resist making critical decisions in the heat of the moment. Instead, I urged her to remain calm, reflect, understand the situation, and then rethink her approach before acting. At first, she struggled to adopt this practice. It wasn't easy for someone so accustomed to being in defense mode. But slowly and steadily, Kyla embraced this new way of thinking.

Watching her transformation was remarkable. Kyla became one of the most reliable and loving leaders I've ever worked with. She learned to balance authority with empathy and strength with vulnerability. Her relationships with her subordinates improved dramatically, as did her ability to lead with authenticity.

I'll never forget the day management announced my transfer to another station. Kyla, the same person who had once been so difficult to approach, broke down in tears. She begged management not to move me, expressing how much she was going to miss me. In that moment, I realized just how far Kyla had come—not just as a leader but as a person. Her tears were a testament to the walls she had torn down and the connections she had built.

Kyla's journey is a profound lesson about leadership and humanity. Beneath the surface of her tough exterior was a heart yearning for connection, healing, and growth. Her rough and raw upbringing had undoubtedly shaped her leadership style, but it didn't define her future. With guidance and support, Kyla redefined herself, becoming an incredible leader and an even better human being.

Another glaring example of this amplification is Elon Musk, whose leadership style is as polarizing as his personality. His leadership style is a direct reflection of his personality—intensely driven, visionary, and unrelenting in his pursuit of excellence. While these qualities have undoubtedly contributed to the success of Tesla, SpaceX, and his other ventures, they have also presented significant challenges for those working under his leadership. His approach highlights the double-edged sword of amplification in leadership: what makes a leader great can also make them difficult to follow.

Musk's ability to articulate and pursue a bold vision is one of his most defining traits. He has consistently set out to solve problems that others deemed impossible, such as mass-market electric vehicles, commercial space travel, and even brain-computer interfaces. His visionary leadership has not only reshaped industries but has also inspired countless individuals to believe in the power of technological progress. His unwavering commitment to long-term goals, such as making humanity a multi-planetary species, serves as a driving force behind his enterprises.

However, this visionary approach comes at a cost. Musk's tendency to set ambitious—some might say unrealistic—

deadlines has led to immense pressure within his organizations. His companies operate in an environment where the expectation to deliver groundbreaking results is relentless. Employees often find themselves caught between innovation and burnout, as Musk's urgency does not always align with practical timelines. His belief in pushing the limits of human capability is admirable, but it also creates an atmosphere where failure is not an option.

Musk thrives on disruption and innovation, always seeking to challenge the status quo. His approach to problem-solving is unorthodox, often disregarding traditional industry practices in favor of radical experimentation. This mindset has allowed him to introduce revolutionary products, from the Tesla Model S to reusable rockets. He fosters a culture of innovation where risk-taking is encouraged, and employees are pushed to think beyond conventional boundaries.

However, this relentless drive can sometimes border on recklessness. Musk's impatience with bureaucracy and traditional business structures has led to hasty decision-making. His impulsive nature is evident in his public statements and management decisions, which sometimes create unnecessary chaos within his organizations. His frequent clashes with regulatory bodies and unpredictable leadership style have led to lawsuits, controversies, and internal upheavals.

Musk exemplifies the paradox of amplification in leadership—his strengths and weaknesses are two sides of the same coin. His ability to push boundaries and demand excellence has led to remarkable achievements, but it has also created an environment where only a select few can endure the intensity of his leadership. Those who can match his work ethic and embrace his vision find themselves at the forefront of history-making advancements. Those who cannot keep up are often left behind.

His leadership style underscores a fundamental truth: leaders do not fundamentally change as they ascend; rather, their existing traits become magnified. Musk was always an intense, driven, and visionary individual—his leadership simply amplified these characteristics on a larger scale. For better or worse, he remains an embodiment of his own philosophy: "If something is important enough, you do it even if the odds are not in your favor."

Unpacking the Past: How childhood scars and experiences shape leaders.

Much of what defines a leader's style can be traced back to their formative years, Warren Bennis said. Childhood experiences, family dynamics, and societal influences create a blueprint for how you interact with the world. These experiences shape not only your personality but also how you approach conflict, decision-making, and relationships—core components of leadership.

At a very early age, Kyla Sanders struggled with trusting her emotion. When she stepped into leadership, this fear manifested as micromanagement. Her co-workers constantly criticized her work, leaving her with a hidden deep-seated fear of failure. Rather than empowering her team, Kyla hovered over their shoulders, inadvertently stifling their creativity. Her leadership style wasn't born from the demands of the role but from the echoes of her childhood.

If you picture Kyla's story keenly, it's obvious Leadership doesn't implant new traits into you; it magnifies what's already there. If you're a naturally empathetic person, that empathy will shine through in your leadership style. If you're prone to self-doubt, that doubt will shadow your decisions. Leadership amplifies your inner world and projects it onto your external reality.

On the flip side, consider Andrew Adams, a tech entrepreneur whose early years were marked by financial instability. Andrew Adams' journey into the world of technology entrepreneurship was neither straightforward nor predictable.

Born into a family that faced significant financial hardship, Andrew's early years were defined by the constant stress of economic instability. His parents, hardworking but financially constrained, taught him the value of resourcefulness and resilience. These lessons were not imparted through deliberate instruction but rather through lived experience—Andrew watched as his parents made sacrifices, adapted to challenges, and found creative ways to make ends meet. These formative experiences shaped the man he would become, instilling in him an unshakable belief in perseverance and self-sufficiency.

As Andrew grew older, his interest in technology became apparent. He saw computers and software not just as tools but as opportunities—pathways to a future where he could transcend the limitations of his upbringing. Without the resources to enroll in prestigious coding boot camps or acquire expensive equipment, he taught himself to program using secondhand computers and free online resources. His natural aptitude for problem-solving, combined with his relentless determination, enabled him to develop a small but innovative software application while still in college. This project, which began as a side hustle, eventually gained traction and laid the foundation for what would become his first startup.

Andrew's company was born in a cramped apartment, fueled by long nights of coding, strategic networking, and an almost obsessive commitment to success. His leadership was driven by an unwavering conviction that no obstacle was insurmountable. To him, setbacks were merely stepping stones to greater achievements. This mindset propelled his company forward, attracting investors who admired his tenacity and a growing team that believed in his vision. However, this same mindset also began to reveal a potential flaw: Andrew struggled to understand why others did not always share his level of resilience.

He expected his employees to operate with the same level of urgency and personal sacrifice that had defined his own journey. Late nights, minimal pay in the early stages, and an all-consuming commitment to work were, in his eyes, necessary ingredients for success. He believed that if he could endure the hardships of building a company from the ground up, then so could everyone else. This belief, however, clashed with the realities of a diverse workforce with different backgrounds, motivations, and personal circumstances.

The Challenge of Empathy

Andrew's struggles with empathy did not stem from a lack of care but rather from a deep-rooted perspective shaped by his past. To him, adversity had been a proving ground—a necessary crucible that had forged his character. When employees expressed concerns about work-life balance, burnout, or the stress of long hours, he found it difficult to relate. He had survived much worse; why couldn't they? This disconnect led to tension within the company, especially as it began to scale.

Early on, when the team was small and composed mostly of like-minded individuals who thrived in high-pressure environments, Andrew's leadership style worked. But as the company grew, so did the diversity of its workforce. Employees with families, those who prioritized mental health, and those who had different approaches to work-life balance began to struggle under his expectations. Turnover rates increased, and morale suffered. For the first time, Andrew faced an issue that could not be solved through sheer grit alone.

The realization that his leadership style was alienating some of his most talented employees came to a head during a company-wide meeting. A senior engineer—one of the company's earliest hires—stood up and expressed what many had been feeling but were too afraid to say: "Andrew, we respect your journey, but not all of us are wired the same way. Just because you toughed it out doesn't mean that should be the standard for everyone."

This moment struck a chord. Andrew, known for his confidence and unwavering resolve, found himself at a crossroads. He could dismiss the concerns and risk further division, or he could reflect on his approach and evolve as a leader. For the first time, he began to consider the possibility that leadership was not just about perseverance and vision— it was also about adaptability and understanding.

Learning to Lead Differently

Andrew took the feedback seriously. He began seeking mentorship from experienced leaders who had successfully navigated similar challenges. He read extensively about leadership styles, emotional intelligence, and organizational behavior. One key realization stood out: leadership was not about imposing one's own experiences onto others but about meeting people where they were and helping them thrive in their own unique ways.

He implemented changes within the company. He introduced flexible work policies, mental health initiatives, and structured mentorship programs that acknowledged different work styles and life circumstances. Rather than viewing these changes as concessions, he saw them as strategic investments in the company's long-term success. He also made a concerted effort to listen—truly listen—to his employees, understanding their motivations, challenges, and needs.

A New Kind of Strength

Through this journey, Andrew did not abandon the principles that had brought him success. He still believed in resilience, determination, and hard work, but he also recognized that these qualities manifested differently in different people. He learned that strength was not just about enduring hardship but also about fostering an environment where people could do their best work without unnecessary struggle.

His transformation as a leader had a profound impact on the company. Productivity improved, turnover rates declined, and the workplace culture became one of support rather than sheer endurance. His ability to balance his core values with a newfound sense of empathy became a defining characteristic of his leadership.

Andrew Adams' story is a testament to the idea that leadership is not about creating something entirely new but about projecting one's past experiences in a way that influences others. His early years of financial instability shaped his resilience, but it was his willingness to grow and adapt that ultimately made him a great leader. His journey highlights an important lesson: while our past shapes us, it does not have to confine us. The best leaders are those who recognize their strengths and weaknesses, who learn from those around them, and who evolve to meet the needs of the people they serve.

Again, his leadership wasn't new—it was a projection of his past.

Your Leadership Shadow: Identifying the patterns you bring to the table.

Leadership is often a reflection of patterns we've carried with us for years. These patterns can be empowering, like resilience and adaptability, or destructive, like insecurity and aggression. The key to becoming a better leader isn't about acquiring new traits; it's about recognizing and reshaping the patterns that no longer serve you.

Every leader operates based on deeply embedded behavioral patterns, whether they realize it or not. These patterns stem from early life experiences, past professional encounters, and deeply held beliefs. Some leaders develop resilience and adaptability due to overcoming adversity, while others may carry insecurities or aggression resulting from unresolved trauma.

For example, individuals who experienced chaotic or unstable environments growing up might unknowingly replicate that chaos in their leadership styles. They may find comfort in high-stakes problem-solving, mistaking constant crisis management for productivity. On the other hand, leaders who have been overlooked or dismissed in their past might seek excessive validation, leading to micromanagement or a lack of confidence in their decision-making abilities.

Recognizing these patterns is the first step toward transformation. It requires self-reflection and a willingness to challenge long-held beliefs. Leaders who fail to identify and reshape unhelpful behaviors often find themselves trapped in cycles that undermine their effectiveness.

The Cycle of Chaos: A Leadership Trap

Some leaders are conditioned to function best in high-pressure, reactive environments. If their upbringing or past experiences were filled with instability, they may subconsciously create similar conditions in their professional lives. Such leaders often believe they perform best under pressure, inadvertently fostering an environment of constant firefighting rather than strategic planning.

These leaders may:

- Delay addressing small issues until they become full-blown crises.
- Make decisions impulsively rather than strategically.
- Reward employees who excel under stress while overlooking proactive problem-solvers.

- Struggle to delegate, believing they must personally manage every challenge.

Over time, this reactive approach erodes team morale and efficiency. Employees may become exhausted from the perpetual state of emergency, leading to burnout, high turnover, and reduced productivity. A leader trapped in this cycle must learn to break free by embracing proactive planning and trusting their team's ability to handle challenges before they escalate.

The Need for Validation: Insecurity in Leadership

Leaders who have experienced neglect, dismissal, or a lack of recognition in the past often carry unresolved emotional baggage into their leadership roles. Their need for validation can manifest in ways that compromise their authority and effectiveness. One common behavior is an overreliance on consensus-building. Instead of making decisive choices, they seek constant approval from their teams, fearing that acting independently might result in rejection or criticism. While collaboration is essential, excessive reliance on group approval can slow decision-making and create an impression of insecurity.

Similarly, these leaders may develop a heightened sensitivity to negative feedback. Because past experiences have conditioned them to equate criticism with personal inadequacy, they may go to great lengths to avoid it. This can lead to conflict avoidance, where they fail to address underperformance, misconduct, or necessary changes within the organization. By prioritizing being liked over enforcing accountability, they risk fostering a culture where standards erode, and team members lose respect for their leadership.

Moreover, their hesitancy to assert authority can create power imbalances, allowing dominant personalities within the team to take control. Employees may begin to question their leader's competence, leading to disengagement or resistance. Ironically, in seeking validation, these leaders may achieve the opposite effect—diminishing their credibility.

Effective leadership requires a balance between emotional intelligence and decisiveness. Leaders must recognize and address their insecurities, ensuring that past experiences do not dictate present leadership behaviors. By cultivating self-awareness and resilience, they can foster trust, respect, and a productive team dynamic.

Some common behaviors of leaders seeking validation include:

- Constantly seeking reassurance from team members or superiors.

- Avoiding unpopular but necessary decisions.

- Becoming overly involved in team dynamics, blurring professional boundaries.

- Reacting defensively to constructive criticism.

This need for external affirmation can be detrimental to leadership effectiveness. Employees respect leaders who display confidence and decisiveness. When leaders overly depend on validation, they risk losing credibility and fostering a culture where team members feel uncertain about decision-making processes. To overcome this, leaders must develop self-assurance, trust their instincts, and understand that effective leadership is not about being liked but about guiding a team toward success.

Transforming Leadership Patterns

Breaking free from unconscious leadership patterns requires leaders to engage in intentional self-awareness practices that challenge their habitual behaviors and cognitive biases. Self-awareness is the foundation of effective leadership, enabling individuals to recognize how their past experiences, emotions, and ingrained beliefs shape their decision-making and interactions. Without this conscious effort, leaders risk perpetuating ineffective patterns that hinder personal growth and organizational success.

One essential practice is regular self-reflection. Leaders should set aside time to analyze their decisions, behaviors, and reactions in various situations. Journaling, for instance, allows them to track patterns and identify recurring triggers that influence their leadership style. Additionally, mindfulness techniques, such as meditation or deep breathing exercises, help leaders remain present, fostering clarity and emotional regulation in high-pressure environments.

Seeking feedback is another critical strategy. Leaders should actively solicit input from peers, mentors, and team members to gain external perspectives on their strengths and blind spots. Constructive feedback creates opportunities for growth by revealing unconscious behaviors that may negatively impact others.

Furthermore, engaging in coaching or leadership development programs can provide structured guidance in breaking limiting patterns. Professional coaches help leaders uncover deep-seated assumptions, challenge ineffective habits, and implement new, conscious behaviors.

Lastly, cultivating a growth mindset is essential. Leaders must embrace continuous learning and adaptability, recognizing that self-awareness is an ongoing process rather than a one-time achievement. By prioritizing intentional self-awareness practices, leaders can transform their approach, fostering a more authentic, empathetic, and effective leadership style

. Here are some ways to reshape unhelpful behaviors:

1. Reflect on Personal Triggers

Understanding what triggers specific behaviors is crucial. Leaders should ask themselves:

- What situations make me feel the need to control everything?
- When do I feel most insecure or defensive in my leadership?
- Are there recurring conflicts or struggles that I contribute to?

Journaling or seeking feedback from trusted mentors can provide insights into these patterns.

2. Embrace Strategic Thinking Over Reactionary Leadership

Leaders who thrive on crisis management must shift toward long-term, strategic thinking. This involves:

- Prioritizing proactive problem-solving rather than reactive decision-making.

- Creating structured systems to prevent constant emergencies.
- Delegating tasks effectively and trusting the team to execute them.

3. Build Confidence in Decision-Making

For leaders who struggle with validation-seeking behaviors, developing self-confidence is essential. This can be done by:

- Establishing clear values and principles to guide decisions.
- Seeking constructive feedback without taking it personally.
- Practicing making tough decisions without over-explaining or seeking excessive approval.

4. Develop Emotional Intelligence

Great leaders cultivate emotional intelligence (EQ) to navigate complex team dynamics. This involves:

- Understanding and managing personal emotions.
- Recognizing emotional triggers in team interactions.
- Communicating with clarity, empathy, and confidence.

5. Seek Professional Development

Leaders can benefit from executive coaching, mentorship, or leadership training programs to refine their approaches. Learning from experienced mentors or engaging in leadership development courses can provide valuable frameworks for improvement.

Leadership is not about acquiring new traits but about recognizing and reshaping existing patterns that no longer serve us. Whether a leader unconsciously creates chaos or seeks constant validation, these patterns can be identified and transformed with self-awareness, strategic thinking, and a commitment to personal growth. By understanding the impact of their past experiences and actively reshaping their behaviors, leaders can create a more stable, effective, and inspiring environment for their teams. The journey toward becoming a better leader begins with the courage to confront and evolve beyond limiting behaviors, ultimately fostering a leadership style that is both authentic and impactful.

The Challenge of Self-Awareness

If leadership reveals who you are, then self-awareness is the flashlight you need to examine the reflection. Without it, you risk becoming a victim of your own habits and blind spots.

Self-awareness allows leaders to distinguish between traits that serve their goals and those that sabotage them.

One effective tool for developing self-awareness is feedback—though it's not always easy to hear. A CEO once told me about an anonymous survey her company conducted. She prided herself on being approachable, but the survey revealed that her employees found her intimidating and unapproachable. It was a gut punch, but it forced her to confront the disparity between how she saw herself and how others experienced her.

Self-awareness isn't just about acknowledging your flaws; it's about actively working to address them. That CEO didn't stop at recognizing her intimidating presence. She began holding regular "ask me anything" sessions, fostering transparency and reducing barriers between her and her team.

Leadership as a Journey of Reflection

The idea that leadership reveals rather than transforms can feel unsettling. It suggests that we carry our baggage into every decision, every conflict, every success. But it also offers hope. If leadership is a mirror, then it's an opportunity—a chance to examine yourself, confront your fears, and rewrite the story you've been living.

Think of leadership not as a role but as a relationship—one that starts with yourself. Before you can effectively lead others, you must lead yourself with honesty and courage. The more you understand your own patterns, the more you can break free from those that hinder your growth.

Consider Oprah Winfrey, whose leadership style is deeply rooted in her personal story. Growing up in poverty and overcoming trauma shaped her into a compassionate and resilient leader. She uses her platform not just to inspire others but to reflect her own journey of self-discovery. Oprah's leadership isn't about adopting a new persona; it's about embracing and amplifying who she is at her core.

Embracing the Mirror

Leadership doesn't come with a manual, but it does come with a mirror. The reflection might not always be flattering, but it's always truthful. The sooner you confront that reflection, the sooner you can begin the real work—not of changing who you are, but of becoming a better version of yourself.

In the chapters ahead, we'll dive deeper into the patterns, fears, and motivations that shape leaders. But for now, remember this: leadership isn't about perfection. It's about progress. It's about recognizing that the mirror doesn't lie and using its reflection to guide your growth.

Leadership may not transform you, but it can reveal the potential you've had all along. The question is—are you ready to look in the mirror?

CHAPTER 2

BROKEN HEARTS, BROKEN CROWN

Leadership is often painted as a glorious crown—a symbol of power, respect, and control. But what we don't talk about is the weight of that crown, especially when the head wearing it is dealing with a broken heart.

Leadership is not just about strategy, decision-making, or inspiring others; it is deeply intertwined with who we are, the scars we bear, and the emotions we suppress. A leader's past—whether filled with violence, neglect, rejection, or insecurity—does not disappear the moment they step into a leadership role. Instead, it subtly weaves itself into their behavior, decision-making, and how they interact with others.

Consider a leader who grew up in an environment of emotional neglect. As a child, they may have learned that love and attention were conditional, earned only through perfection or relentless effort. This experience can manifest in leadership as a relentless pursuit of results, where perfection is demanded from their team, and any sign of failure is met with harsh criticism. The leader is not necessarily cruel; rather, they are reliving their own upbringing, where mistakes equated to a loss of worth. They push their teams harder, not out of malice, but because their own self-worth was once tied to impossible standards.

On the other hand, a leader who experienced violence—whether physical or emotional—may approach leadership with an unconscious need to control their environment. Having grown up in unpredictability, they may fear losing grip on their team or organization, leading them to micromanage, distrust others, or resort to intimidation to maintain order. To them, control feels like safety. Yet, in doing so, they can stifle creativity, crush morale, and foster a culture of fear rather than innovation.

Alternatively, a leader shaped by pain can use their experiences to lead with profound empathy. Those who have endured hardship often possess a unique ability to recognize struggle in others. They may become the kind of leader who listens deeply, understands unspoken frustrations, and advocates for their people because they know what it feels like to be unheard. Their leadership is not just about results but about ensuring no one under their watch experiences the same pain they once did.

The key difference between leaders who perpetuate cycles of pain and those who break them lies in self-awareness. A leader who recognizes how their past influences their present can make conscious choices rather than reacting out of old wounds. They can challenge their inherited behaviors, seek growth, and redefine what leadership means for them.

True leadership is not just about wearing the crown; it is about carrying its weight with wisdom. It is about understanding that leadership magnifies not only our strengths but also our unresolved wounds. The most impactful leaders are not those who pretend they have no scars but those who acknowledge them, learn from them, and use their experiences to lead with authenticity and depth.

Leading with Fear: How growing up around violence breeds aggressive leadership.

The Fear Beneath the Crown

At the core of every aggressive leader is fear. Not the primal fear of danger but the subtle fear of being exposed—of being seen as weak, incapable, or unworthy. For someone who has experienced trauma, especially violence or neglect, leadership can feel like standing on a stage without a script. To shield themselves, they lean into aggression, mistaking it for strength.

Leadership rooted in fear often manifests as control, micromanagement, or outright aggression. Leaders driven by fear are not inherently "bad" leaders; they are simply reacting to the deep-seated insecurities and experiences that shaped them.

Take Sam, a senior manager at a manufacturing company. Sam was raised in an environment where mistakes were punished harshly. His father, a military veteran, believed discipline was the only path to success, often enforcing it with a heavy hand. As a leader, Sam struggled with perfectionism and reacted harshly to his team's mistakes. Employees described him as unapproachable and intimidating, but the truth was that Sam wasn't angry with them—he was terrified of failing. His aggression was a defense mechanism, a way to hide the fear instilled in him as a child.

Anger as a Shield

Anger, when used as armor, serves as a shield against vulnerability, but it ultimately isolates leaders rather than empowering them. Leaders like Sam wield anger as a means of control, believing that by intimidating others, they can command obedience and maintain order. However, this tactic is unsustainable. While fear may drive short-term compliance, it never fosters genuine commitment or trust among team members. Instead, it creates a toxic environment where employees act out of self-preservation rather than shared purpose.

When leaders rely on anger to assert dominance, they fail to acknowledge its corrosive effects. Anger pushes people away, making it difficult for teams to communicate openly, share ideas, or admit mistakes. Employees become more focused on avoiding conflict than on contributing meaningfully. This not only stifles innovation but also breeds resentment and disengagement. Over time, the leader who constantly projects anger will find themselves surrounded by individuals who either mirror their hostility or withdraw entirely. Neither outcome is conducive to a thriving organization.

True leadership requires emotional intelligence—the ability to recognize, understand, and manage emotions in oneself and others. Leaders who acknowledge their vulnerabilities and express emotions constructively cultivate a culture of trust.

Instead of using anger as a shield, effective leaders embrace transparency and accountability, fostering an environment where people feel valued and heard. This creates loyalty, encouraging employees to go beyond their basic duties because they believe in the leader's vision, not because they fear their reaction.

Ultimately, anger is a weak foundation for leadership. It may provide an illusion of power, but it fails to inspire genuine respect. A leader who trades intimidation for empathy, and control for connection, builds a lasting legacy—not through fear, but through trust and collaboration.

Fear-Based Behaviors

Micromanagement: A need to oversee every detail to avoid failure.

Avoidance of Conflict: Fear of confrontation leading to unresolved issues.

Overreaction to Mistakes: Treating errors as personal threats rather than opportunities to learn.

Fear-based leadership takes a toll not just on the leader but also on their team. Employees working under aggressive leaders often feel undervalued, overworked, and emotionally drained. These environments stifle creativity and innovation, replacing collaboration with a culture of compliance.

Therapy and team-building exercises are part of the journey to overcoming fear-based leadership. Leaning to trust your team, delegate effectively, and focus on big-picture goals rather than day-to-day control.

Control Freaks Anonymous: Why fear of losing power leads to micromanagement.

Control is the crutch of a fearful leader—one who prioritizes authority over trust, compliance over collaboration, and rigidity over adaptability. While exerting control might offer temporary relief by creating a sense of order, it is ultimately a destructive force that stifles growth, innovation, and morale.

At its core, excessive control stems from fear—fear of failure, uncertainty, or losing status. Leaders who operate from this mindset believe that by micromanaging every detail, they can eliminate risk. However, this approach creates an environment where employees feel disempowered, hesitant to take initiative, and afraid to voice new ideas. Over time, this erodes motivation and fosters a culture of dependency rather than responsibility.

Organizations thrive on adaptability, creativity, and trust—qualities that controlled environments suffocate. When employees are trusted to make decisions, they develop confidence and a sense of ownership in their work. They become problem-solvers rather than passive executors of orders. However, when control is the dominant force, employees learn to do only what is expected, avoiding risks that could lead to innovation.

Moreover, excessive control damages relationships. Employees begin to see leadership as a force to appease rather than an ally in their professional growth. This weakens loyalty, increases turnover, and ultimately undermines the very stability that control-seeking leaders aim to achieve.

True leadership is about influence, not coercion. Great leaders empower their teams, set clear expectations, and allow space for autonomy. They understand that success is not about eliminating uncertainty but about equipping people with the confidence and skills to navigate it.

In the long run, control is not a strength—it's a liability. Leaders who cling to it may find temporary comfort, but they will always be outpaced by those who embrace trust, flexibility, and shared responsibility.

Tom, the CEO of a growing startup, struggled with delegation. Every decision, no matter how minor, had to go through him. Employees described feeling suffocated, and the company's growth stalled.

Tom's behavior stemmed from a traumatic childhood where he was frequently blamed for his family's financial troubles. Delegating felt like relinquishing control, and relinquishing control felt like inviting disaster.

The Costs of Overcontrol

1. **Employee Disempowerment**: Stifling creativity and autonomy.
2. **Leader Burnout**: Taking on too much leads to exhaustion.
3. **Missed Opportunities**: Focusing on the wrong priorities.

Solutions for Letting Go

Tom eventually worked with an executive coach to identify his triggers and build trust with his team. By delegating tasks and focusing on strategic decisions, he regained his energy and helped his company thrive.

The Fight Within: Overcoming internal battles to lead with courage.

Healing the Broken Crown

Many leaders battle internal conflicts—doubts, fears, and unresolved pain—that shape their external behavior. These internal struggles often stem from personal experiences, past failures, or deep-seated insecurities that manifest in leadership styles, decision-making, and interactions with others. The good news is that leaders with broken hearts don't have to stay broken. Healing begins with acknowledging the pain and understanding how it influences behavior. This isn't about erasing the past but learning to navigate its effects with self-awareness and intention.

One of the first steps toward healing as a leader is self-reflection. Leaders must be willing to examine their past experiences and identify the sources of their emotional wounds. This could be childhood trauma, professional setbacks, betrayal, or feelings of inadequacy that have followed them into their leadership roles. By recognizing these underlying issues, leaders can begin to make sense of their reactions, biases, and tendencies.

For example, a leader who experienced abandonment or neglect may struggle with trust, leading them to micromanage their team out of fear of being let down. Another leader who has faced repeated criticism may develop a defensive leadership style, resisting feedback and rejecting differing opinions. These behaviors are often subconscious, but their impact on team dynamics and organizational culture is profound. A leader's unresolved pain can create an environment of fear, instability, or disengagement, limiting the potential of both the leader and their team.

Consider David, a CFO at a large corporation, struggled with imposter syndrome. Despite his qualifications, he constantly doubted his abilities, leading him to overcompensate by demanding perfection from his team.

David's self-doubt stemmed from a father who never acknowledged his achievements, He said. Leadership magnified this insecurity, making every decision feel like a test he might fail.

However, true leadership requires the courage to confront these struggles head-on. This means seeking self-awareness, whether through journaling, coaching, therapy, or mentorship. When leaders understand their pain, they can begin to shift their responses from reactive to intentional. Instead of acting out of fear, they can lead with empathy and clarity, making decisions that are driven by wisdom rather than emotional baggage.

Healing also involves vulnerability. Contrary to traditional notions of strong leadership, vulnerability does not signify weakness. Instead, it fosters genuine connections and trust. When leaders acknowledge their struggles and openly work toward self-improvement, they model authenticity for their teams. Employees are more likely to respect and support a leader who is human and relatable rather than one who projects an unbreakable facade.

Moreover, healing is not a solitary journey. Leaders who surround themselves with a strong support system—whether mentors, trusted colleagues, or professional counselors—can gain valuable perspective and encouragement. These relationships provide a safe space for leaders to express doubts, receive constructive feedback, and develop healthier leadership habits.

Leaders who embrace healing become catalysts for change within their organizations. When they operate from a place of self-awareness and emotional intelligence, they foster cultures of psychological safety, resilience, and growth. They empower their teams by recognizing strengths, offering meaningful support, and encouraging open dialogue. Instead of perpetuating cycles of pain and dysfunction, they break the pattern, paving the way for healthier, more sustainable leadership.

Leadership is not about being flawless; it is about being willing to evolve. Leaders who confront and heal their internal wounds become stronger, more compassionate, and more effective. Healing does not erase the past, but it transforms it into a source of wisdom, allowing leaders to navigate challenges with greater self-awareness and intention. The journey is ongoing, but for those who embark on it, the reward is not only personal growth but the ability to lead others with authenticity and purpose.

Understanding the Internal Fight

1. **Imposter Syndrome**: Feeling unworthy despite evidence of competence.

2. **Fear of Vulnerability**: Hiding emotions to appear strong.

3. **Perfectionism**: Using high standards to mask self-doubt.

Leaders with broken hearts may carry their pain into their roles, but they also carry the potential to grow. Recognizing the fear beneath the crown is the first step toward leading with authenticity and compassion.

The Weight Of Not Been Enough

Leadership is often associated with confidence, decisiveness, and unwavering self-belief. Leaders are expected to be the anchors in turbulent times, the visionaries who inspire teams, and the decision-makers who chart the course toward success. Yet, behind the polished facade of many accomplished leaders lies an unspoken struggle: the persistent feeling of not being "enough." This self-doubt, often referred to as impostor syndrome, can quietly erode a leader's effectiveness, influencing their decisions, relationships, and overall impact.

The weight of leadership responsibility can be overwhelming. Leaders are constantly scrutinized, their actions analyzed, and their decisions questioned. While external pressure is an inherent part of leadership, the internal battle of self-doubt can be far more debilitating. It manifests in second-guessing decisions, hesitating to take bold actions, or seeking excessive validation from others. A leader who feels inadequate may struggle to trust their instincts, leading to indecisiveness and missed opportunities. When self-doubt becomes pervasive, it diminishes confidence and breeds insecurity, creating a vicious cycle where fear of failure prevents the pursuit of innovation and progress.

One of the most damaging aspects of self-doubt in leadership is its impact on relationships. Leaders who feel inadequate may overcompensate by adopting authoritarian tendencies, micromanaging their teams to mask their own insecurities. Conversely, they may become excessively accommodating, avoiding difficult conversations or decisions for fear of being perceived as incompetent. Both extremes can undermine trust and respect, leading to disengagement among team members. Employees look to leaders for guidance and stability, and when they sense uncertainty or insecurity, it can erode morale and confidence within the organization.

The source of this self-doubt is often deeply rooted in personal history, past failures, or a fear of being exposed as inadequate. Many leaders, despite their accomplishments, struggle with perfectionism, believing that any mistake is a reflection of their incompetence. The pressure to meet unrealistic expectations—whether self-imposed or external—can create a persistent sense of never measuring up. Social comparison further exacerbates these feelings, as leaders often measure their success against others, overlooking their unique strengths and contributions.

However, self-doubt does not have to be a silent saboteur. The most effective leaders acknowledge and confront their insecurities rather than allowing them to dictate their actions. Developing self-awareness is key—understanding personal triggers, recognizing negative self-talk, and reframing failure as an opportunity for growth. Seeking mentorship and support can also provide perspective, reminding leaders that they are not alone in their struggles.

Authenticity in leadership is more valuable than projecting an illusion of perfection. Leaders who embrace their vulnerabilities foster an environment where openness and resilience thrive. By modeling self-acceptance and continuous learning, they empower their teams to do the same. True leadership is not about eradicating self-doubt but learning to lead despite it. The ability to navigate uncertainty with humility and adaptability is what distinguishes great leaders from merely competent ones. The journey of leadership is not about attaining an unshakable sense of confidence, but rather about developing the courage to move forward, even when doubt lingers in the background.

Imposter Syndrome on Steroids: When leaders doubt their worth.

Impostor syndrome, the persistent belief that one's success is undeserved, is common among high achievers. It's the inner voice that whispers, "You don't belong here," or, "They'll find out you're a fraud." For leaders, impostor syndrome can be paralyzing, casting a long shadow over their ability to make decisions or take risks. In this section, we'll uncover the roots of impostor syndrome, its manifestations in leadership, and how to confront and overcome it.

Janet was the Chief Operating Officer of a multinational corporation. Her resume boasted Ivy League degrees and years of successful leadership experience. Yet, every time she walked into a boardroom, she felt like an imposter. "I've just been lucky," she'd tell herself, minimizing her hard work and talent. Janet's self-doubt made her second-guess her decisions and avoid taking bold actions, fearing they'd expose her perceived incompetence.

Her impostor syndrome stemmed from her upbringing. As the youngest of five siblings in a competitive household, she was constantly compared to her more accomplished brothers and sisters. Even as an adult, she couldn't shake the feeling that she was an accidental success.

Janet's turning point came during an executive coaching session where her coach asked her to write down her accomplishments, then objectively compare them to what she thought an "impostor" would achieve. Seeing her achievements on paper helped her realize they weren't a result of luck—they were earned through grit and skill.

Manifestations in Leadership

- Overworking to Prove Worth: Leaders with impostor syndrome often push themselves—and their teams—

to the brink, believing that visible effort validates their position.

- Avoiding Risks: Fear of failure keeps them in their comfort zones, hindering innovation.

- Micromanaging: They don't trust others to deliver, believing the burden of success rests solely on their shoulders.

Strategies to Overcome Impostor Syndrome

- Reframe Your Narrative: Replace "I got lucky" with "I prepared and delivered."

- Celebrate Small Wins: Acknowledge achievements to reinforce self-confidence.

- Seek Feedback: Trusted colleagues can provide objective insights into your strengths.

Emotion Overload: How low self-esteem fuels reactive leadership.

Emotional leadership, when balanced with self-awareness and intelligence, can be a powerful asset. Leaders with high emotional intelligence can connect with their teams, foster a positive work culture, and inspire motivation. However, when emotions are unchecked and dominate decision-making, they can lead to erratic or reactionary leadership that ultimately harms the organization and its people.

One of the primary pitfalls of unchecked emotional leadership is the influence of insecurity. Leaders who feel "not good enough" often allow their emotions—whether fear, anger, or sadness—to take control of their actions and decisions. This can result in defensive behavior, impulsivity, or avoidance of difficult but necessary conversations. Rather than leading with clarity and vision, they may make decisions based on personal validation or emotional relief rather than strategic thinking.

Fear-based leadership, for example, manifests when leaders are constantly worried about failure, judgment, or rejection. They may avoid taking risks, stifle innovation, or micromanage their teams to maintain a sense of control. A fearful leader might also resist delegating tasks, fearing that others will outperform them, thereby undermining trust and team cohesion. Over time, this fear-driven approach creates a stagnant environment where employees feel restricted and disengaged.

Similarly, anger-driven leadership can be destructive. Leaders who allow frustration or resentment to dictate their actions often create a culture of hostility and intimidation. Instead of addressing issues with logic and professionalism, they may lash out at employees, blame others for setbacks, or make hasty decisions based on temporary emotions. This type of leadership erodes trust, lowers morale, and increases employee turnover. It also blinds leaders to valuable feedback and alternative solutions that could improve the organization.

On the other hand, leaders who are overly influenced by sadness or self-doubt may struggle with assertiveness and decision-making. When a leader is consumed by feelings of inadequacy, they may hesitate to take a firm stance on important issues, defer to others excessively, or seek constant reassurance. This lack of confidence can create confusion among team members and result in a lack of direction for the organization. Employees may feel uncertain about expectations and lose confidence in the leader's ability to guide them effectively.

A key characteristic of strong leadership is the ability to acknowledge emotions without being controlled by them. Emotional intelligence allows leaders to recognize their feelings, assess their impact, and respond thoughtfully rather than react impulsively. Self-regulation, a core component of emotional intelligence, helps leaders maintain composure in stressful situations and make informed, strategic decisions that align with long-term goals rather than immediate emotional impulses.

To cultivate balanced emotional leadership, leaders must practice self-reflection and emotional regulation. This includes seeking feedback, engaging in mindfulness or stress-management techniques, and fostering a growth mindset. By developing resilience and self-awareness, leaders can harness their emotions as a source of empathy and motivation rather than letting them dictate their actions.

In conclusion, emotional leadership is not inherently bad; it becomes detrimental when emotions override logic, strategy, and self-awareness. Great leaders understand that emotions are valuable but should be managed with discipline. By striking a balance between emotional intelligence and rational decision-making, leaders can inspire trust, maintain stability, and drive their organizations toward sustained success.

Victor was a team leader in a customer service department. Known for his passionate speeches and charismatic presence, he had the potential to inspire his team. However, his insecurity about his qualifications—he had been promoted despite lacking a college degree—made him defensive. Anytime his ideas were challenged, he reacted emotionally, turning constructive feedback into personal attacks.

Victor's emotional outbursts created a culture of fear. Team members stopped sharing ideas or offering feedback, afraid of triggering his temper. It wasn't until Victor attended a leadership retreat and heard similar stories from other leaders that he realized the damage he was causing. With the help of a mentor, he learned techniques to pause and reflect before reacting, transforming his emotional energy into empathy and understanding.

Manifestations in Leadership

- Overreaction to Criticism: Taking feedback personally rather than constructively.

- Emotion-Driven Decisions: Letting anger, fear, or sadness overshadow logic.

- Inconsistent Leadership: Mood swings creating instability within the team.

Strategies to Balance Emotions

- Practice Emotional Regulation: Techniques like mindfulness or journaling can help leaders process their feelings before reacting.

- Develop a Support System: Trusted advisors can provide perspective and grounding.

- Focus on Facts: Use data to inform decisions, balancing emotion with logic.

Accountability Is Not a Dirty Word: Breaking the victim mindset.

Leadership is often tested in moments of failure, yet some leaders struggle to take responsibility when things go wrong. Instead of owning their mistakes, they frame themselves as victims of circumstance or shift the blame onto their teams. This behavior is not merely a leadership flaw but often stems from deep-seated feelings of inadequacy and a fragile sense of self-worth. By deflecting accountability, these leaders create a psychological shield that protects them from confronting their own perceived shortcomings. However, this approach ultimately undermines both their credibility and their team's ability to grow and improve.

One of the primary reasons leaders avoid taking responsibility is fear—fear of failure, fear of judgment, and fear of exposing their limitations. Many leaders operate under the belief that they must appear infallible to command respect and authority. When failure occurs, they perceive it as a direct threat to their competence and self-image. Instead of addressing the problem constructively, they resort to externalizing blame, positioning themselves as victims of uncontrollable circumstances or the inefficiency of their subordinates.

This pattern of behavior is often rooted in a lack of self-awareness. Leaders who struggle with feelings of inadequacy may have developed coping mechanisms that include deflecting blame and avoiding critical self-reflection. They may have experienced environments where admitting mistakes was punished rather than seen as an opportunity for growth. As a result, they internalize the idea that acknowledgment of failure equates to weakness. Over time, this avoidance strategy becomes a habitual response, making it difficult for them to accept responsibility even when it is clearly warranted.

The impact of blame-shifting leadership extends beyond the individual leader. It creates a toxic work environment where accountability is discouraged, and trust erodes. When employees see their leader refusing to own up to mistakes, they become disillusioned and disengaged. A culture of fear develops, where individuals hesitate to take initiative or innovate because they know they may be scapegoated if things go wrong. This stifles creativity and limits the organization's potential for growth and success.

Moreover, leaders who frame themselves as victims often miss valuable learning opportunities. Failure, when approached with accountability, serves as a powerful teacher. By analyzing what went wrong and making necessary adjustments, organizations can improve efficiency and avoid repeating mistakes. Leaders who refuse to engage in this process not only stunt their own development but also hinder the evolution of their teams and organizations.

A more effective leadership approach embraces accountability as a strength rather than a weakness. Leaders who acknowledge their role in failures demonstrate humility and resilience. They create an environment where team members feel safe to voice concerns, take calculated risks, and learn from setbacks. This, in turn, fosters a culture of continuous improvement and trust.

To break the cycle of blame and victimization, leaders must develop emotional intelligence and self-awareness. They should actively seek feedback, engage in self-reflection, and cultivate a mindset that views failure as a stepping stone rather than a threat. True leadership is not about avoiding mistakes but about taking ownership of them, learning, and guiding others toward collective success. By embracing responsibility, leaders build credibility, inspire loyalty, and drive meaningful progress within their organizations.

Anna was the manager of a retail store. Whenever sales targets weren't met, she'd blame her team for underperforming. When employee turnover increased, she pointed fingers at corporate policies. Anna's refusal to accept accountability eroded trust among her employees, who felt demoralized and undervalued.

Anna's victim mentality traced back to her early career, where she was often scapegoated by her supervisors. To protect herself, she developed a habit of deflecting blame. A turning point came when her regional manager confronted her directly, challenging her to own her mistakes and lead by example. Through coaching and self-reflection, Anna began to shift her perspective, recognizing that leadership required accountability, even when it was uncomfortable.

Manifestations in Leadership

- Blaming Others: Avoiding personal responsibility for failures.

- Excuses Over Solutions: Focusing on reasons for failure rather than fixing the problem.

- Erosion of Trust: Employees lose respect for leaders who don't take accountability.

Strategies to Overcome Victim Mentality

- Own Your Mistakes: Acknowledge failures openly and focus on solutions.

- Build Resilience: Develop a mindset that views challenges as opportunities for growth.

- Encourage Team Collaboration: Involve your team in problem-solving to foster trust and shared accountability.

The weight of not being enough is a heavy burden for any leader to carry. Whether it manifests as impostor syndrome, emotional decision-making, or a victim mentality, it can undermine even the most talented individuals. But the weight can be lifted. By acknowledging these patterns, leaders can begin the journey toward self-awareness and growth, creating space for authenticity, accountability, and connection. True leadership isn't about being perfect; it's about being willing to learn and evolve.

CHAPTER 3

COMPETENCE VS. COMPLAINTS: THE LEADERSHIP TUG-OF-WAR

Leadership is a balancing act between capability and critique. At its best, leadership serves as a proactive and empowering force, where leaders use their skills to uplift others, drive results, and cultivate a culture of growth.

True leadership is not merely about authority or titles; it is about influence, responsibility, and the ability to inspire. Leaders who demonstrate competence and emotional intelligence foster trust, encourage innovation, and create an environment where individuals feel valued and motivated to contribute their best efforts. However, when leadership falters, the dynamics shift, and what was once a force for progress can deteriorate into a culture of blame and defensiveness.

Competence is the foundation upon which effective leadership stands. A leader's ability to navigate challenges, make informed decisions, and guide a team through uncertainty determines their impact. When competence is strong, leaders exude confidence without arrogance, ensuring their teams feel secure in their direction. They set clear expectations, provide resources, and offer constructive feedback that enables their teams to grow. They understand that leadership is not about knowing everything but about fostering an environment where learning and collaboration thrive. These leaders acknowledge their own limitations and seek to improve themselves just as much as they encourage their teams to do so.

However, when competence falters—whether due to inexperience, lack of knowledge, or external pressures—the temptation to redirect attention outward can become overwhelming. Instead of addressing personal or organizational shortcomings, ineffective leaders may resort to criticism, blame, and deflection. This defensive approach erodes trust and morale, creating a toxic work culture where employees operate in fear rather than inspiration. Instead of fostering problem-solving, such leaders stifle creativity and risk-taking, as employees become more focused on avoiding blame than on achieving excellence.

The gap between competence and complaints defines the leadership experience for many. Those who rise above the noise of complaints and embrace growth and accountability distinguish themselves as true leaders. They recognize that leadership is a continuous journey of self-improvement, adaptability, and resilience. These individuals face challenges head-on, learn from failures, and demonstrate the humility needed to accept constructive criticism. They prioritize solutions over scapegoating and take responsibility for their decisions. When mistakes occur, they use them as learning opportunities rather than excuses to shift blame.

On the other hand, leaders who fall into the trap of blaming others risk losing trust, respect, and ultimately their own potential. Once a leader becomes known for deflecting responsibility, their credibility diminishes. Employees disengage, innovation stalls, and overall performance suffers. Without accountability, leadership becomes transactional rather than transformational, reducing leaders to mere managers who enforce rules rather than inspire change.

True leadership requires a commitment to growth, not just for oneself but for the entire team. It demands emotional intelligence, self-awareness, and the courage to confront weaknesses. Leaders who embrace these qualities foster a culture of trust, where individuals feel empowered to contribute, take risks, and drive meaningful change. In contrast, those who dwell in the realm of blame and critique will find themselves isolated, ineffective, and ultimately unsuccessful. Leadership is not about being perfect; it is about being accountable, learning, and consistently striving to uplift those around you.

The Blame Game: When incompetence masks as criticism.

Leadership is often seen as the pinnacle of responsibility—leaders are expected to inspire, guide, and make critical decisions that shape the future of their teams and organizations. However, they are also human, susceptible to errors, miscalculations, and blind spots. The real measure of leadership is not in the avoidance of mistakes but in how leaders respond when they inevitably fall short. Unfortunately, rather than embracing accountability, some leaders resort to deflecting responsibility, blaming external factors, subordinates, or circumstances beyond their control. This tendency to shift blame has far-reaching consequences, eroding trust, damaging team morale, and stunting organizational growth.

The Temptation to Deflect

Leadership comes with immense pressure. The expectation to consistently perform at high levels can feel overwhelming, making failure seem like an unacceptable outcome. When things go wrong, some leaders instinctively seek to preserve their reputation by shifting blame to others—whether it be employees, market conditions, or upper management. This defensive response often stems from insecurity, fear of losing authority, or an unwillingness to acknowledge personal flaws.

Deflection can take many forms. Some leaders subtly undermine their teams by suggesting that underperformance is due to a lack of effort from employees rather than ineffective leadership. Others point fingers at factors such as budget constraints, competitors, or even the attitudes of their workforce. While external challenges do play a role in operational difficulties, a leader's refusal to own their part in a failure prevents meaningful solutions from being developed.

The Consequences of Blame-Shifting

The most immediate consequence of deflecting responsibility is the erosion of trust. Employees respect leaders who demonstrate honesty and integrity, even in failure. When a leader consistently shifts blame, it creates an environment of fear and uncertainty, where employees feel vulnerable to scapegoating. Over time, this damages morale, discourages initiative, and fosters a culture of avoidance rather than accountability.

Moreover, deflection prevents the leader from addressing the real problem. If a team fails to meet expectations, an accountable leader would analyze what went wrong, assess whether they provided adequate resources and guidance, and implement corrective measures. A blame-shifting leader, however, remains blind to their own shortcomings, perpetuating the same mistakes and reinforcing a cycle of dysfunction.

Another consequence is the stifling of innovation. When leaders refuse to take ownership of failures, employees become reluctant to take risks or experiment with new ideas. They fear that any misstep will be met with punishment rather than constructive feedback. This discourages creative problem-solving and inhibits progress within the organization.

The Power of Accountability

True leadership requires the courage to own mistakes and learn from them. Leaders who acknowledge their missteps not only gain the respect of their teams but also foster an environment where accountability is valued at all levels.

Instead of creating a culture of blame, they cultivate one of continuous improvement, where failures are seen as opportunities for growth rather than reasons for punishment.

By embracing accountability, leaders set a powerful example. They demonstrate resilience, emotional intelligence, and the ability to adapt—qualities that inspire confidence and loyalty. More importantly, they position themselves as problem-solvers rather than victims of circumstance, leading their teams with authenticity and purpose.

In the end, leadership is not about being infallible. It is about being responsible, learning from setbacks, and using those lessons to build stronger, more effective teams. The leaders who thrive are not those who point fingers but those who reflect, adapt, and rise above their failures with integrity.

Jeremy was the supervisor of a maintenance team at a manufacturing plant. When production delays started occurring, he immediately blamed his team for inefficiency. He complained that his staff wasn't motivated enough and lacked the discipline to meet deadlines. Behind closed doors, Jeremy vented to his peers, convinced the problem wasn't him but the "lazy" workers under him.

What Jeremy failed to recognize was his role in the issue. He rarely communicated clear expectations and had no system for tracking progress. A particularly bold team member finally approached him and said, "Jeremy, we don't know what you want from us. Every day it feels like you change your priorities." That feedback stung, but it was the wake-up call he needed. With the help of his HR department, Jeremy learned to improve his planning and communication skills. Over time, he became a leader who inspired trust rather than resentment.

Manifestations of the Blame Game

- Deflecting Accountability: Leaders shift blame to others to protect their egos.

- Eroding Trust: Teams grow disengaged when they feel scapegoated.

- Missed Opportunities for Growth: Leaders who blame others fail to address their own skill gaps.

How to Shift From Complaints to Competence

- Acknowledge Weaknesses: Accept that you don't have all the answers and commit to improving.

- Seek Honest Feedback: Encourage your team to point out areas where you can improve.

- Focus on Problem-Solving: Instead of dwelling on what went wrong, prioritize finding solutions.

Micromanaging vs. Mastery: Insecurity on Display.
Micromanaging often stems from insecurity. Leaders who feel unqualified to lead may overcompensate by exerting excessive

control over their teams. However, this behavior undermines trust, stifles creativity, and hampers productivity.

Sarah Kamara was the CEO of a growing tech startup. Her hands-on approach had been essential in the early days, but as the company expanded, it became a liability. Sarah micromanaged every aspect of her team's work, from approving minor design changes to rewriting emails. Her team began to resent her interference, and talented employees started leaving the company.

Sarah's behavior was rooted in fear. She worried that if she let go of control, her company would fail. During a leadership workshop, she learned the importance of delegation and trust. A turning point came when she decided to let her marketing team run a campaign without her input. The campaign was a success, and Sophia realized that empowering her team didn't diminish her leadership—it strengthened it.

Signs of Micromanagement in Leadership

- Obsessive Oversight: Constantly checking and rechecking work.
- Fear of Delegation: Reluctance to let others take responsibility.

- Low Team Morale: Employees feel undervalued and disengaged.

How to Move From Micromanagement to Mastery

- Delegate With Confidence: Assign tasks based on team members' strengths and trust their abilities.

- Focus on Big-Picture Goals: Shift your energy from day-to-day details to strategic planning.

- Invest in Training: Equip your team with the skills they need to succeed independently.

From Surviving to Thriving: Building competence one challenge at a time.

Some leaders rely on complaints as a defense mechanism. Instead of addressing challenges head-on, they make excuses, blame external factors, or focus on what's wrong rather than what's possible. This behavior stifles growth—for both the leader and their organization.

The Psychological Comfort of Complaints

Leaders who default to complaints often find solace in the illusion that they are powerless against their circumstances. By blaming external factors—such as corporate policies, industry trends, or team inefficiencies—they absolve themselves of accountability. This mindset provides temporary relief but ultimately prevents them from taking the proactive steps necessary for change. Over time, this attitude fosters a culture of inaction, where challenges are seen as insurmountable rather than as opportunities for growth and innovation.

Raj was the manager of a boutique hotel. Whenever guests left negative reviews, he found a reason to justify it. If the complaint was about room cleanliness, he blamed the housekeeping staff. If it was about slow service, he pointed to high turnover rates in the hospitality industry. Over time, Raj's constant excuses began to wear thin with his team and his superiors.

The Ripple Effect on Organizational Culture

When a leader consistently engages in complaint-driven leadership, it creates a domino effect within the organization. Employees take cues from their leaders, and if complaints become the norm, the workforce may adopt a similar mindset. Rather than striving for solutions, employees may resort to blaming colleagues, processes, or external conditions for their struggles. This erodes morale, reduces productivity, and discourages innovation. In such environments, problem-solving takes a back seat to finger-pointing, and progress stagnates.

Missed Opportunities for Growth

Every challenge presents an opportunity for improvement, but leaders who focus solely on what's wrong miss the chance to evolve. Instead of using setbacks as learning experiences, they reinforce a victim mentality that limits personal and organizational advancement. Great leaders understand that setbacks are inevitable, but they view them as stepping stones rather than stumbling blocks. They ask, "What can we do differently?" instead of "Why does this always happen to us?" This shift in perspective leads to innovation, resilience, and long-term success.

Shifting from Complaints to Solutions

Leaders who wish to break free from the cycle of complaints must cultivate a mindset of ownership and accountability. This begins with self-awareness—recognizing when they are falling into a pattern of blame and consciously redirecting their focus toward actionable solutions. Instead of dwelling on limitations, they must ask empowering questions:

- What is within my control to change?
- How can I turn this challenge into an opportunity?
- What lessons can be learned from this situation?
- Who can I collaborate with to develop a viable solution?

One day, a senior executive visited the hotel and sat down with Raj. "Do you realize how many excuses you've made in this conversation?" she asked. That moment of clarity forced Raj to reflect on his leadership approach. With coaching, he began shifting his focus from what couldn't be done to what could. He implemented new training programs for his staff, improved communication channels, and began taking responsibility for guest satisfaction. The hotel's ratings improved, and so did Raj's reputation as a leader.

By fostering a culture of problem-solving, leaders inspire their teams to think creatively, take initiative, and embrace challenges with confidence. This shift not only strengthens the leader's own capabilities but also enhances the overall resilience and adaptability of the organization.

The Cost of Complaints in Leadership

- Stagnation: Complaints prevent leaders from seeking solutions and driving progress.

- Loss of Credibility: Teams lose faith in leaders who focus on problems rather than possibilities.

- Negative Culture: A complaint-driven leader fosters a blame-oriented environment.

How to Cultivate a Growth Mindset

- Reframe Challenges as Opportunities: Instead of dwelling on what's wrong, focus on what can be improved.

- Take Ownership: Accept responsibility for outcomes, both good and bad.

- Lead by Example: Model a solution-oriented attitude for your team.

The tension between competence and complaints is a defining challenge for leaders. Complaints often mask deeper insecurities, whether it's fear of failure, lack of confidence, or resistance to change. By addressing these insecurities, leaders can shift their focus from critiquing others to improving themselves. True leadership is about growth—acknowledging weaknesses, seeking solutions, and empowering others to do the same.

Complaints may provide momentary relief, but they do little to foster growth or success. Leaders who use complaints as a defense mechanism risk creating a stagnant, disengaged workforce that sees obstacles as permanent roadblocks. On the other hand, those who embrace challenges as opportunities for innovation and improvement drive their organizations toward lasting success. The key to effective leadership lies not in highlighting problems, but in having the courage and initiative to seek solutions.

CHAPTER 4

AGGRESSION VS ASSERTIVENESS

L eadership is, at its core, a balancing act. Among the most delicate balances is the one between aggression and assertiveness. While both behaviors may outwardly look like strength, their underlying motivations and outcomes couldn't be more different. Aggression seeks to dominate, often rooted in fear, insecurity, or a desire for control. Assertiveness, on the other hand, is guided by self-assurance and respect—respect for oneself, others, and the shared goal. Leaders who confuse these two modes of interaction risk alienating their teams, stifling collaboration, and, ultimately, failing in their mission to inspire and guide others.

Aggression is a reactive force that stems from an emotional impulse. It often manifests as hostility, intimidation, or coercion. Aggressive leaders tend to push their agendas forward without considering alternative perspectives, silencing dissenting voices through fear or manipulation. They may achieve short-term compliance, but their approach fosters resentment, disengagement, and resistance. Over time, aggressive leadership erodes trust, discourages creativity, and diminishes team morale. Employees in such environments often feel undervalued and unheard, leading to high turnover rates, lower productivity, and overall dissatisfaction.

Conversely, assertiveness is a proactive and empowering leadership style. Assertive leaders communicate their needs, opinions, and expectations clearly and confidently without undermining or demeaning others. They understand that leadership is not about overpowering subordinates but about fostering an environment where mutual respect thrives. These leaders actively listen to their teams, encourage dialogue, and remain open to constructive criticism. By promoting transparency and accountability, they create a culture of trust and collaboration.

One of the key differences between aggression and assertiveness lies in emotional intelligence. Aggressive leaders react impulsively, allowing frustration or fear to dictate their actions. Assertive leaders, however, exercise self-awareness and emotional control. They recognize their triggers and channel their energy into constructive solutions rather than destructive confrontations. This emotional intelligence enables them to navigate conflicts effectively, finding resolutions that benefit all parties involved instead of resorting to intimidation or coercion.

Another distinction is in the long-term impact on organizational culture. Aggressive leadership breeds a toxic work environment where employees feel undervalued and operate under constant stress. The pressure to conform without question stifles innovation, as individuals become hesitant to propose new ideas or challenge existing processes. Assertive leadership, on the other hand, nurtures an atmosphere where employees feel empowered to contribute, take initiative, and grow professionally. Such environments foster high levels of engagement, motivation, and performance.

To cultivate assertiveness, leaders must practice active listening, clear communication, and emotional regulation. They must also develop the ability to stand firm on important matters while remaining open to feedback and adaptation. Setting boundaries is another crucial aspect of assertive leadership. An effective leader knows when to say no, when to push forward, and when to compromise—always with respect and confidence.

Ultimately, true leadership is not about exerting dominance but about inspiring others. The most effective leaders understand that strength is not measured by force but by influence, and that true influence comes from authenticity, confidence, and respect. By choosing assertiveness over aggression, leaders not only foster a healthier workplace but also drive sustainable success for their teams and organizations.

The Fine Line: Why aggression isn't authority.

Aggression in leadership often stems from deep-seated fears or insecurities. Many leaders believe that being aggressive will earn them respect, command authority, or assert their dominance in the room. While aggression can yield short-term compliance, its long-term consequences are usually destructive—leading to distrust, resentment, and even rebellion.

Aggression in leadership is often a reaction to internal anxieties. Leaders who feel uncertain about their capabilities, fear losing control, or struggle with imposter syndrome may resort to aggression as a defensive mechanism. They believe that projecting dominance will mask their vulnerabilities and establish their authority. However, authority built on fear rather than trust is inherently unstable. Employees and team members may comply out of fear, but their engagement and motivation will dwindle over time.

Aggressive leadership fosters a toxic work environment. When employees feel constantly berated, threatened, or demeaned, they are less likely to take initiative or voice innovative ideas. Fear stifles creativity and collaboration, both of which are essential for organizational growth. Moreover, employees subjected to aggression often experience higher levels of stress, which can lead to burnout, increased absenteeism, and high turnover rates. No organization thrives when its workforce operates under perpetual fear.

One of the most damaging aspects of aggressive leadership is the erosion of trust. Trust is the foundation of any effective team, and when leaders rule with aggression, they create an "us versus them" dynamic. Employees become more concerned with self-preservation than with the success of the team or organization. This leads to disengagement, passive resistance, and, in extreme cases, active rebellion. Workers may begin to intentionally undermine leadership, contribute the bare minimum, or seek opportunities elsewhere.

Another consequence of aggression in leadership is its negative impact on company culture. Employees often mirror the behavior of their leaders. If a leader is aggressive, it sets a precedent for others to act similarly, creating a culture of hostility and competition rather than cooperation and mutual respect. This kind of environment discourages teamwork and makes it difficult to retain top talent. Talented employees, especially those who have options, are unlikely to stay in an organization where they feel undervalued or constantly attacked.

In contrast, effective leadership is built on respect, empathy, and communication. Leaders who are firm but fair earn genuine respect from their teams. They encourage dialogue, provide constructive feedback, and create an atmosphere where employees feel safe to take risks and grow. Assertiveness, rather than aggression, is the key to maintaining authority while fostering a positive work environment. Assertive leaders set clear expectations, hold employees accountable, and communicate their needs without belittling or intimidating others.

Ultimately, leadership is about influence, not intimidation. While aggression may produce immediate compliance, it does not inspire loyalty or long-term commitment. True leaders understand that their role is to guide, support, and empower their teams. By focusing on emotional intelligence and self-awareness, leaders can replace aggression with confidence and foster an environment where both employees and organizations thrive.

Darren was the operations manager at a mid-sized logistics company. Known for his fiery temper, he believed his aggressive style kept employees on their toes. He regularly raised his voice during team meetings, publicly called out individuals for mistakes, and micromanaged projects to the point of suffocating creativity.

One day, his team missed a major delivery deadline due to a miscommunication between departments. Darren exploded in anger, berating employees for their "incompetence" in front of colleagues. Unbeknownst to him, one of his top-performing team members had been quietly planning her resignation for months because she felt emotionally drained by his leadership style.

Eventually, Darren's department experienced high turnover rates and declining morale. His aggression, which he had mistaken for strength, was revealed to be the root of his team's dysfunction. It wasn't until his HR director sat him down and showed him anonymous employee feedback that Darren began to confront his own insecurities and fear of losing control.

Manifestations of Aggression in Leadership

- Verbal Outbursts: Yelling or using harsh language to establish authority.

- Overpowering Decisions: Making unilateral decisions without consulting the team.

- Public Criticism: Using shame as a tool for compliance.

Strategies to Address Aggressive Tendencies

- Identify Triggers: Reflect on situations that provoke aggressive reactions.

- Seek Feedback: Encourage employees to share how they perceive your behavior.

- Practice Emotional Regulation: Use techniques like mindfulness or journaling to manage stress.

Speaking Up Without Blowing Up: Building trust through assertive communication.

Assertiveness is one of the most misunderstood traits in leadership and communication. It is often mistaken for aggression by those who view any form of directness as hostility, and it is dismissed as weakness by those who equate authority with dominance. However, true assertiveness is neither of these extremes. It is the golden mean between passivity and aggression—a state where confidence and empathy coexist in perfect harmony.

Assertiveness is the ability to express one's thoughts, needs, and boundaries clearly and respectfully while also considering the perspectives of others. Unlike passivity, which involves suppressing one's voice to avoid conflict, and aggression, which involves imposing one's will without regard for others, assertiveness allows individuals to communicate effectively without violating the dignity of others. It is an essential skill in both personal and professional relationships, fostering respect, understanding, and mutual cooperation.

One of the most common misconceptions about assertiveness is that it is synonymous with aggression. This confusion arises because both assertive and aggressive individuals are often direct in their communication. However, the key difference lies in intent and delivery. An aggressive person seeks to dominate, control, or belittle others to get their way, often using intimidation or coercion. In contrast, an assertive person communicates with confidence but remains respectful, ensuring that their words and actions do not demean or harm others.

On the other end of the spectrum, some view assertiveness as a form of weakness. This perspective is particularly prevalent in hierarchical or highly competitive environments where dominance is mistaken for leadership. In such settings, individuals who choose to balance confidence with empathy may be perceived as indecisive or lacking authority. However, this view fails to recognize that the most effective leaders are those who inspire collaboration rather than command obedience. An assertive leader does not need to resort to fear or coercion; instead, they cultivate trust and respect by listening actively, addressing concerns, and making well-reasoned decisions that benefit the collective.

The benefits of assertiveness are far-reaching. In the workplace, assertive communication leads to clearer expectations, reduced misunderstandings, and a healthier work culture. Employees who feel empowered to express their ideas and concerns without fear of retaliation are more engaged, innovative, and productive. Similarly, in personal relationships, assertiveness fosters honesty and respect, allowing for open discussions that strengthen bonds rather than creating resentment.

Developing assertiveness requires practice and self-awareness. It involves setting clear boundaries, using "I" statements to express needs without blaming others, and actively listening to different perspectives. It also requires the ability to manage emotions effectively, ensuring that confidence does not turn into arrogance and empathy does not lead to self-sacrifice.

In a world where communication is often either too aggressive or too passive, assertiveness stands out as the ideal approach. It allows individuals to navigate conflicts with poise, advocate for themselves without alienating others, and build relationships based on mutual respect. By embracing assertiveness, we not only become better communicators and leaders but also foster environments where both confidence and empathy thrive.

Maria was a newly promoted team leader in a marketing agency known for its high-pressure environment. She inherited a team notorious for internal conflicts and lackluster performance. Unlike her predecessor—who had ruled with an iron fist—Maria adopted an assertive approach. She set clear expectations, invited open dialogue, and addressed conflicts directly but respectfully.

When one team member, Greg, repeatedly missed deadlines, Maria didn't berate him in front of the team. Instead, she scheduled a one-on-one meeting to understand the root of the problem. Greg revealed he was struggling with time management and requested additional support. Maria provided him with resources and followed up regularly, which resulted in a dramatic improvement in his performance.

Within a year, Maria's team had not only resolved its internal tensions but also achieved record-breaking results. Her assertiveness created a culture of mutual respect, accountability, and growth.

Key Attributes of Assertive Leaders

- Clarity: Communicating expectations and goals transparently.

- Empathy: Balancing firmness with genuine concern for others.

- Accountability: Taking responsibility for decisions while encouraging the same in others.

Developing Assertiveness in Leadership

- Practice Active Listening: Show genuine interest in others' perspectives before asserting your own.

- Use "I" Statements: Express your needs and concerns without blaming others.

- Set Boundaries: Be firm but respectful when addressing unacceptable behavior.

The Cost of Confusion: When Aggression Masquerades as Assertiveness

Many leaders mistake aggression for assertiveness, believing that pushing their will onto others is a sign of strength or decisiveness. However, these two traits—aggression and assertiveness—are fundamentally different, and understanding the distinction is crucial for effective leadership.

Aggression typically involves behaviors that are forceful, hostile, or combative. An aggressive leader might resort to harsh language, intimidation, or even threats to get their way. The key characteristic of aggression is that it disregards the rights, feelings, or perspectives of others in favor of achieving one's own goals. This approach often stems from insecurity, fear, or an overwhelming desire to control situations. While aggression might seem effective in the short term, it usually undermines the relationship between the leader and their team. Employees may feel threatened, disrespected, or undervalued, which can lead to anxiety and diminished trust.

Assertiveness, on the other hand, is about standing up for one's own needs, ideas, or boundaries in a way that is respectful of others. An assertive leader communicates clearly, listens actively, and makes decisions confidently without resorting to coercion or manipulation. Assertiveness is rooted in self-respect and mutual respect, and it fosters an environment where open communication and collaboration can thrive. Assertive leaders are able to express their views or decisions with conviction, while still being open to feedback and input from others. This creates a healthier, more inclusive work environment that encourages team members to share their thoughts and contribute to problem-solving.

The confusion between aggression and assertiveness often results from an overemphasis on results and a lack of understanding about the importance of emotional intelligence. Aggressive leadership may seem to produce immediate results, particularly in high-pressure situations. However, over time, this leads to burnout, resentment, and a disengaged workforce. Employees who feel belittled or threatened are less likely to take initiative or collaborate effectively. In contrast, assertive leaders tend to inspire loyalty and trust, which enhances overall productivity and employee satisfaction.

Building trust through assertiveness is essential for long-term success. Trust is the foundation of strong relationships, both between leaders and their teams, and among team members themselves. When employees trust their leader, they feel safe to express their ideas and concerns, knowing they will be heard and respected. This, in turn, leads to a more engaged and motivated workforce, which directly impacts the organization's performance.

Moreover, aggressive leadership often contributes to high employee turnover, as individuals who feel undervalued or intimidated by their leader are more likely to leave in search of a healthier work environment. Conversely, assertive leaders, who respect the autonomy and contributions of their team, foster loyalty and reduce turnover.

Ultimately, the distinction between aggression and assertiveness comes down to respect. Assertive leaders acknowledge the needs and perspectives of others, while aggressive leaders prioritize their own agenda at the expense of those around them. By cultivating assertiveness, leaders can create a positive work culture where individuals feel empowered to contribute, collaborate, and succeed together. It's an essential shift for any leader who seeks to inspire trust, foster teamwork, and achieve sustainable success.

Jackie, a director at a nonprofit organization, prided herself on being assertive. She believed her no-nonsense approach was necessary to drive results in a fast-paced environment. However, her team often felt bullied and intimidated by her communication style. Jackie interrupted colleagues during meetings, dismissed dissenting opinions, and imposed unrealistic deadlines.

One day, an anonymous employee survey revealed the truth: most of her team felt undervalued and disrespected. Jackie was shocked. "I thought I was being assertive, not aggressive," she confessed to a leadership coach. With guidance, she began to shift her approach—learning to listen more, acknowledge others' contributions, and frame her demands in a collaborative way. Over time, her team's trust in her leadership grew, and so did their productivity.

Red Flags of Aggression Disguised as Assertiveness

1. **Overconfidence**: Mistaking domineering behavior for decisiveness.

2. **Dismissiveness**: Ignoring feedback or alternative perspectives.

3. **Short-Term Wins, Long-Term Losses**: Achieving goals at the expense of relationships and morale.

Steps to Clarify Your Leadership Style

- **Reflect on Outcomes**: Are your team's results sustainable, or are they driven by fear?

- **Seek External Perspectives**: Ask mentors or peers for honest feedback on your approach.

- **Balance Strength With Sensitivity**: Ensure your firmness is rooted in respect, not control.

Transforming Aggression Into Assertiveness.

The journey from aggression to assertiveness is one of self-awareness, humility, and intentionality. By recognizing aggressive tendencies and committing to change, leaders can unlock their full potential and create environments where both they and their teams thrive. This transformation requires a conscious effort to balance personal confidence with respect for others, ensuring that communication is both effective and empowering rather than domineering or confrontational.

Aggression in leadership often stems from deep-seated habits, past experiences, or even a misconception that authority equates to dominance. While aggressive behavior may yield short-term results by forcing compliance, it ultimately erodes trust, morale, and collaboration. Leaders who operate with aggression may experience resistance from their teams, reduced innovation, and increased turnover. Recognizing these drawbacks is the first step in shifting towards assertiveness.

Assertiveness, on the other hand, is the ability to express one's thoughts, needs, and expectations clearly and confidently while maintaining respect for others. It is rooted in emotional intelligence, where leaders balance self-assurance with empathy, ensuring that their words and actions foster an inclusive and constructive atmosphere. Unlike aggression, which imposes force, assertiveness encourages dialogue and cooperation.

Emma, a senior executive at a tech company, was known for her aggressive leadership style. Her sharp criticism and high demands drove results, but they also created a culture of fear and burnout. One day, her closest colleague resigned, citing Emma's behavior as the primary reason. "You're brilliant, but you're impossible to work with," he told her bluntly.

Devastated, Emma decided to seek help. She enrolled in an executive coaching program and began practicing mindfulness to regulate her emotions. She also implemented a feedback system to encourage honest communication within her team. Over time, Emma transformed her approach—becoming a leader who inspired loyalty rather than fear.

Steps to Transform Aggression Into Assertiveness

Develop Self-Awareness: The first step in transformation is recognizing personal triggers and patterns of aggressive behavior. This requires honest self-reflection and, in some cases, seeking feedback from peers and subordinates. Identifying moments when communication becomes forceful or intimidating helps leaders understand the underlying causes, whether it be stress, frustration, or fear of losing control.

Cultivate Emotional Intelligence: Emotional intelligence (EQ) plays a crucial role in this transformation. By developing self-regulation, leaders can manage their impulses, respond rather than react, and approach situations with a calm demeanor. Practicing mindfulness and active listening allows them to remain present in conversations, reducing the likelihood of aggressive responses.

Embrace Humility and Open Communication: Assertive leaders recognize that leadership is not about asserting dominance but about fostering a collaborative environment. They remain open to feedback, admit mistakes, and value diverse perspectives. This humility strengthens relationships and creates a culture of trust and mutual respect.

Practice Constructive Communication: Shifting from aggression to assertiveness requires changes in verbal and non-verbal communication. Using "I" statements instead of "you" accusations can make a significant difference. For example, saying "I feel concerned when deadlines are missed" rather than "You never meet deadlines" encourages discussion rather than defensiveness. Maintaining a calm tone, controlled body language, and steady eye contact further reinforces a leader's confidence without intimidation.

Set Clear Expectations and Boundaries: Assertive leaders establish clear expectations while allowing room for discussion. They communicate boundaries with respect, ensuring that their teams understand the rationale behind decisions without feeling threatened or undervalued.

Lead by Example: Leaders must model the behavior they wish to see. By demonstrating assertiveness in action, they encourage their teams to adopt similar communication styles, leading to a healthier, more productive work environment.

The Impact of Assertive Leadership

Leaders who successfully transition from aggression to assertiveness experience profound improvements in team dynamics. Trust replaces fear, collaboration flourishes, and employees feel empowered to contribute ideas without fear of retaliation. Productivity increases as teams function with mutual respect and clarity. Additionally, leaders themselves experience lower stress levels, as assertive communication fosters problem-solving rather than conflict escalation.

The journey from aggression to assertiveness is not an overnight change but a continuous process of growth and refinement. Through self-awareness, emotional intelligence, and intentional communication, leaders can harness their strengths in a way that uplifts rather than suppresses. In doing so, they unlock their full leadership potential, creating workplaces that thrive on respect, engagement, and shared success.

The emotional balancing act

Leadership is commonly framed through the conventional lenses of strategy, vision, and decision-making. However, an often overlooked yet equally vital element is the emotional dimension of leadership. While intellect and logical analysis are critical for making informed decisions, emotions—the leader's own and those of others—serve as an invisible, yet powerful force in shaping a team's dynamics, trust, and overall performance. Every leadership challenge, interaction, and decision involves navigating this emotional terrain. The capacity to manage these emotional complexities becomes the distinguishing factor between successful and ineffective leadership.

Emotional balancing act lies the leader's ability to empathize with their team while remaining decisive. Empathy is the bridge that connects a leader to their people, fostering trust and understanding. When a leader can identify with the struggles and aspirations of their team members, they create an environment of support and mutual respect. This emotional bond cultivates loyalty, encourages open communication, and ultimately, boosts morale. However, empathy alone is not enough. A leader must also be able to make decisions—often tough and unpopular ones—without being paralyzed by the emotional impact on others. A leader must balance the weight of empathy with the clarity of purpose, ensuring that while team members' feelings are valued, the needs of the organization and its goals take precedence.

Vulnerability, too, plays a pivotal role in effective leadership. It is easy to fall into the trap of projecting invulnerability, believing that a leader must always be strong, unflappable, and resolute. Yet true strength often lies in the ability to show vulnerability—acknowledging when one doesn't have all the answers, admitting mistakes, and being open to feedback. This fosters an atmosphere where team members feel safe to express their own concerns, ideas, and challenges. However, vulnerability must be carefully balanced with the leader's role as a pillar of stability. It is important that a leader not become overwhelmed by their emotions or the emotional needs of others to the point of losing their capacity to lead with clear direction and focus.

Self-awareness is another critical emotional skill for leaders. A deep understanding of one's emotional triggers, biases, and patterns allows a leader to respond thoughtfully, rather than react impulsively. This emotional intelligence creates the space for better decision-making and helps avoid the pitfalls of emotional overreaction. Yet, being attuned to one's own emotions is only half of the equation. A truly effective leader must also be aware of the emotions of their team. This requires a sensitivity to body language, tone of voice, and other non-verbal cues that reveal how others are feeling. This heightened awareness empowers the leader to adjust their approach as needed, providing the right support, encouragement, or direction at the right time.

The challenge of emotional balancing in leadership is not an optional skill—it is essential. When the emotional elements are neglected or mismanaged, leadership can quickly devolve into a chaotic and reactive process. The team may feel disconnected, disengaged, and unsupported, which can result in missed opportunities, low morale, and high turnover. On the other hand, when a leader successfully manages their emotional landscape, they lead with clarity, purpose, and authenticity. They inspire trust, motivate their team, and create a culture of collaboration and excellence. In this equilibrium, a leader can guide their team not only toward achieving organizational goals but also toward fostering an environment where individuals feel valued, understood, and empowered. This balance of head and heart becomes the foundation of truly transformative leadership.

The Trap of Overidentifying with Others

Empathy is often hailed as a superpower in leadership. And rightly so—it builds trust, strengthens relationships, and fosters collaboration. However, unchecked empathy can lead to overidentification with others' emotions, blurring the line between support and emotional enmeshment. Leaders who fall into this trap risk losing objectivity, taking on emotional burdens that aren't theirs, and ultimately burning out.

Overidentification occurs when leaders absorb the emotions of their team members to such an extent that they begin to experience those emotions as their own. While the ability to understand and validate another person's feelings is crucial, it becomes problematic when leaders internalize those struggles, losing their ability to maintain a balanced perspective. Instead of providing clarity and solutions, they may become overwhelmed, react emotionally rather than strategically, and make decisions based on sentiment rather than reason.

One of the biggest dangers of overidentification is emotional exhaustion. Leadership often requires difficult decisions, such as disciplining employees, addressing performance issues, or making budget cuts. If a leader is too emotionally entangled, they may struggle to make tough calls, fearing the emotional distress it may cause others. This can lead to decision paralysis or ineffective leadership, where emotions override necessary action. Over time, this emotional burden accumulates, leading to burnout, decreased effectiveness, and even personal resentment toward the role or the people they lead.

Moreover, overidentification can distort the leader's ability to see the bigger picture. When a leader is overly absorbed in one employee's struggles, they may unintentionally neglect the needs of the broader team. Their perspective becomes skewed, and instead of fostering fairness and accountability, they may inadvertently enable underperformance by excusing behavior that requires correction. This can create workplace imbalances, fostering resentment among other team members who may perceive preferential treatment.

Another significant drawback of excessive empathy is the erosion of professional boundaries. While leaders should create a safe and supportive environment, they must also maintain the distinction between professional and personal responsibilities. Employees need leaders who can provide guidance, support, and mentorship—not individuals who become so emotionally intertwined that they lose their leadership stance. If a leader assumes the role of a therapist or a personal confidant, it becomes difficult to make unbiased decisions that align with organizational goals.

To avoid this trap, leaders must practice empathetic detachment—a balance between understanding others' emotions while maintaining their own emotional resilience. This means recognizing and acknowledging team members' challenges without internalizing them. Strategies such as active listening, emotional self-regulation, and setting clear professional boundaries can help leaders provide support while remaining objective. Additionally, cultivating self-awareness through mindfulness or coaching can help leaders recognize when they are absorbing too much emotional weight.

Ultimately, the most effective leaders are those who can empathize without losing themselves in others' struggles. By maintaining this balance, leaders can sustain their emotional energy, make objective decisions, and create an environment where both they and their teams can thrive.

Consider Lisa, a customer service manager, prided herself on being an empathetic leader. Her team felt comfortable sharing their struggles with her—personal and professional. One employee, Sarah, frequently confided in Lisa about her financial difficulties and family issues. Lisa, wanting to help, often worked late to cover for Sarah, handled her workload, and even lent her money.

While Lisa's intentions were pure, the constant emotional burden left her drained. Her productivity suffered, and she began resenting Sarah, even though she had willingly taken on the extra weight. Eventually, Lisa realized that her overidentification wasn't helping Sarah grow; it was enabling her to avoid accountability.

Key Lessons:

Healthy Empathy vs. Overidentification: Empathy involves understanding and supporting others without absorbing their emotions or responsibilities.

Boundaries Matter: Setting emotional and professional boundaries is not a lack of empathy; it's a sign of emotional intelligence.

Practice Detached Compassion: Show understanding without taking ownership of others' feelings.

Empower, Don't Enable: Encourage team members to solve their own problems with your guidance, not your intervention.

Vulnerability Without Weakness.

For decades, vulnerability was considered a liability in leadership. But modern research and stories of transformational leaders reveal a different truth: vulnerability is a strength when wielded wisely. It builds authenticity, deepens trust, and fosters a culture of openness. The challenge lies in striking a balance—showing enough vulnerability to connect with others without undermining your authority or credibility.

Mark, the CEO of a tech startup, faced a major product launch failure that threatened the company's survival. During an all-hands meeting, instead of delivering a polished speech, Mark admitted his own feelings of fear and disappointment. He shared how the failure had affected him but also expressed his belief in the team's ability to recover and innovate.

Mark's honesty inspired the team. Employees felt empowered to share their own ideas and concerns without fear of judgment. Together, they developed a new strategy that turned the company around. Mark's vulnerability, rather than weakening his position, made him a more relatable and respected leader.

Key Lessons:

Controlled Vulnerability: Being open about struggles or mistakes can build connection, but it must be paired with a clear path forward to inspire confidence.

Strength in Authenticity: Vulnerability is not about oversharing; it's about being honest while maintaining focus and direction.

How to Be Vulnerable Without Losing Authority:

Share Selectively: Reveal emotions or challenges that are relevant to the team's context.

Combine Vulnerability with Vision: Pair honesty about struggles with a clear plan of action.

Self-Awareness Without Self-Absorption.

Self-awareness is the cornerstone of emotional intelligence. It enables leaders to understand their triggers, biases, and strengths. However, too much focus on oneself can lead to self-absorption, where a leader's personal growth overshadows their responsibility to others. Balancing self-awareness with a broader perspective is key to effective leadership.

lex, a regional sales manager, was committed to personal development. He attended leadership workshops, read books, and constantly sought feedback. While his self-awareness improved, his team began to feel neglected. Alex was so focused on his own growth that he failed to notice the declining morale and unmet needs within his team.

When Alex finally paused to evaluate his leadership impact, he realized he had been leading in isolation. He shifted his approach, involving his team in his learning journey and focusing on their development as much as his own. The change revitalized his team's trust and performance.

Key Lessons

Balance is Key: Self-awareness should inform leadership decisions, not become the sole focus.

Lead Outward, Not Inward: Use personal growth to enhance team growth, not as an end in itself.

Building Balanced Self-Awareness

Regular Reflection: Evaluate how your behavior impacts others.

Seek Diverse Feedback: Encourage input from peers, mentors, and subordinates.

Managing Emotional Contagion.

Emotions are highly contagious, especially in leadership settings where a leader's mood and reactions directly influence their team. Whether positive or negative, emotions spread rapidly, shaping workplace culture, employee engagement, and overall productivity. Understanding and managing emotional contagion is not just an individual responsibility but a critical leadership skill that determines an organization's success.

The Science Behind Emotional Contagion

Emotional contagion refers to the subconscious transmission of emotions between individuals. Studies in psychology and neuroscience reveal that humans mirror the emotions of those around them through facial expressions, vocal tones, and body language. This phenomenon occurs due to mirror neurons, which cause people to instinctively replicate the emotional states of others. Leaders, by virtue of their position, have a greater impact on their team's emotional environment. Their expressions of enthusiasm, frustration, or stress can ripple through the organization, affecting team morale and performance.

The Impact of Emotional Contagion on Leadership

A leader's emotional state sets the tone for the workplace. Positive emotions, such as enthusiasm, confidence, and optimism, create an environment where employees feel motivated, engaged, and willing to collaborate. In contrast, negative emotions, such as anger, frustration, or anxiety, can demoralize a team, increase stress levels, and diminish productivity. Employees take cues from their leaders, and if a leader consistently exhibits negativity, the team is likely to mirror that behavior, leading to a toxic work environment.

A leader's ability to regulate emotions is particularly crucial during challenging situations. In times of crisis or uncertainty, employees look to their leaders for stability and reassurance. If a leader remains calm and solution-focused, it fosters a sense of security and confidence among employees. Conversely, if a leader reacts with panic or aggression, it exacerbates the stress within the team, leading to poor decision-making and decreased morale.

Strategies for Managing Emotional Contagion

Effective leaders recognize the power of emotional contagion and take deliberate steps to manage their own emotions while influencing their team's emotional climate positively. Here are some key strategies:

Self-Awareness and Emotional Regulation – Leaders must develop self-awareness to recognize their emotional triggers and manage their responses. Practicing mindfulness, self-reflection, and emotional intelligence helps leaders maintain control over their emotions, preventing negative feelings from spilling over onto their teams.

Modeling Positive Behavior – Leaders should consciously exhibit the attitudes and behaviors they want their team to emulate. Demonstrating resilience, optimism, and empathy encourages employees to adopt similar mindsets, fostering a supportive and productive workplace culture.

Open and Transparent Communication – Addressing challenges with honesty and clarity can prevent unnecessary stress and anxiety among team members. Leaders should communicate challenges with a balanced perspective, focusing on solutions rather than dwelling on problems.

Creating a Supportive Environment – Encouraging a culture of psychological safety, where employees feel comfortable expressing concerns and ideas, helps mitigate the spread of negativity. Providing support through active listening and constructive feedback reinforces trust and motivation.

Encouraging Work-Life Balance – A leader's acknowledgment of employee well-being significantly impacts team morale. Promoting healthy work habits and recognizing the importance of breaks and time off helps maintain emotional equilibrium within the team.

Emotional contagion is a powerful force in leadership, capable of shaping workplace dynamics and organizational success. Leaders who proactively manage their emotions and cultivate a positive emotional environment can inspire their teams, enhance performance, and foster long-term success. By embodying emotional intelligence, practicing self-awareness, and promoting a supportive culture, leaders can harness the power of emotional contagion to drive both individual and collective growth within their organizations.

CHAPTER 5

BUILDING YOUR LEADERSHIP DNA

Leadership is often mistaken for a job title or a specific set of skills, yet it transcends these simplistic definitions. It is a way of being a living embodiment of values, beliefs, and behaviors that influence others. Leadership is not about the position you hold or the accolades you achieve, but about how you show up every day, how you engage with those around you, and the impact you have on them. This essence of leadership is rooted in your Leadership DNA—a unique combination of your personal experiences, choices, and growth that shape who you are as a leader.

Your Leadership DNA is not something you are born with or receive from external sources; it is continuously forged over time. It is shaped by your experiences, both positive and negative, by the people you've encountered, and by the lessons you've learned along the way. These experiences become the building blocks of your leadership style, and your ability to navigate challenges, inspire others, and make decisions is a direct reflection of this DNA. While some leadership traits may come naturally, others require introspection, intentional development, and consistent effort.

At the core of Leadership DNA are your values, emotional intelligence, resilience, and vision. Your values determine what you stand for and guide your decision-making. They act as your moral compass, ensuring that your actions align with the kind of leader you aspire to be. Emotional intelligence—the ability to recognize, understand, and manage your emotions, as well as those of others—forms the foundation of strong interpersonal relationships and effective communication.

Resilience enables you to weather setbacks, bounce back from failure, and keep moving forward, regardless of the obstacles in your path. Vision is what gives your leadership purpose and direction, inspiring others to follow and contribute toward a shared goal.

But the most powerful element of Leadership DNA is self-awareness. Knowing who you are, your strengths, weaknesses, biases, and motivations, allows you to lead with authenticity. When you are deeply in touch with yourself, your leadership becomes grounded in honesty and integrity. It becomes easier to make decisions that are aligned with your values, and you become more empathetic and understanding in your interactions with others. Leadership is not about perfection; it's about showing up as the truest version of yourself and creating an environment where others feel empowered to do the same.

Building your Leadership DNA is not a linear process. It is a journey of continuous learning and growth, marked by moments of self-discovery, vulnerability, and reflection. It requires unearthing the layers of conditioning, biases, and fears that influence your behavior and consciously choosing to align your actions with the kind of leader you want to become. Along the way, you will encounter challenges that force you to confront your limitations and expand your capabilities. This is the crucible in which your leadership identity is forged, and each experience will refine and redefine your DNA.

Authentic leadership begins when you stop trying to imitate others or follow someone else's blueprint for success. Instead, you embrace your own unique path, grounded in your personal values, experiences, and aspirations. It is only through this self-acceptance and commitment to growth that you will be able to inspire and influence others in meaningful ways. When you lead from a place of authenticity, your leadership resonates with those around you, creating an environment of trust, collaboration, and mutual respect. In the end, Leadership DNA is not just about how you lead others—it's about how you lead yourself.

Why Leadership DNA Matters

Imagine a house built without a foundation—it may look impressive on the outside, but it crumbles at the first sign of stress. Similarly, leadership without a strong foundation of self-awareness and authenticity is unsustainable.

Leadership DNA is what keeps you grounded during crises, resilient in the face of setbacks, and consistent in your principles. It allows you to lead with integrity, because your decisions are rooted in your core values, not external pressures or fleeting emotions.

When leaders lack clarity about their Leadership DNA, they often adopt borrowed styles, relying on imitation rather than authenticity. This not only creates internal conflict but also erodes trust with their teams. People can sense when a leader is acting out of alignment with their true self. Conversely, leaders who embody their Leadership DNA radiate confidence and consistency, inspiring loyalty and respect.

The Building Blocks of Leadership DNA

Core Values: Your guiding principles that influence every decision you make.

Emotional Intelligence: Your ability to understand and manage your own emotions while empathizing with others.

Resilience: Your capacity to bounce back from adversity and adapt to change.

Vision: Your ability to see the bigger picture and inspire others toward a shared goal.

Take the story of Priya, an engineer-turned-CEO of a renewable energy company. Priya started her career with a singular focus: solving technical problems. But when she transitioned to leadership, she realized that her success depended not on her technical expertise but on her ability to inspire and align people.

Priya's first leadership challenge came during a major project delay. Her team was disheartened, and morale was at an all-time low. Initially, she tried to emulate the tough, stoic style of her previous boss, issuing directives and pushing for results. But it backfired—her team grew more disengaged.

Frustrated, Priya took a step back and reflected on her core values: collaboration, innovation, and trust. She decided to lead differently. Instead of issuing orders, she facilitated open conversations, admitted her own frustrations, and asked for the team's input. By aligning her actions with her values, Priya not only turned the project around but also earned the trust and loyalty of her team.

Key Lessons

Authentic leadership begins with self-awareness.

Aligning your actions with your core values builds trust and influence.

Leadership DNA is not fixed; it evolves with intention and reflection.

Unearthing the Foundation

Before you can build your Leadership DNA, you must uncover it. This involves examining your past experiences, understanding your values, and identifying the beliefs that shape your decisions. Your blueprint is already within you; it just needs to be brought to light.

How to Discover Your Blueprint

> ➤ Reflect on your past experiences and the lessons they've taught you.

> ➤ Identify your core values and how they influence your decisions.

> ➤ Seek feedback from trusted colleagues or mentors.

Breaking Free from Conditioned Patterns.

Leadership is often viewed as the ability to inspire, guide, and make decisive choices. However, many leaders unknowingly operate within invisible constraints—conditioned patterns formed through childhood experiences, cultural expectations, or past professional encounters. These patterns, deeply ingrained in their psyche, can manifest as blind spots, reactive tendencies, or even self-sabotaging behaviors that limit their potential. Breaking free from these conditioned responses requires courage, self-awareness, and a commitment to intentional change.

Understanding Conditioned Patterns

Conditioned patterns are automatic responses to situations, shaped by past experiences and reinforced over time. For example, a leader who grew up in an environment where mistakes were harshly criticized may develop an aversion to risk-taking, fearing failure rather than embracing it as a learning opportunity. Similarly, someone raised in a hierarchical culture may struggle with delegation, believing that authority should not be shared. These patterns often operate beneath the surface, influencing decision-making, communication, and leadership style without conscious awareness.

One of the most significant dangers of conditioned patterns is their ability to create blind spots. A leader may assume they are making rational decisions when, in reality, they are reacting based on past wounds or deeply held fears. For instance, a leader who has experienced betrayal in a previous role might struggle with trust, inadvertently micromanaging their team rather than empowering them. Recognizing these blind spots is the first step toward transformation.

The Role of Self-Awareness in Breaking Free

Self-awareness is the cornerstone of personal and professional growth. Without it, leaders remain trapped in cycles of reaction rather than intentional action. Developing self-awareness requires reflection, feedback, and a willingness to confront uncomfortable truths about oneself.

Journaling, meditation, or working with a mentor or coach can help leaders uncover patterns they were previously blind to. Additionally, seeking honest feedback from colleagues and employees provides valuable external perspectives. The goal is to recognize automatic reactions—whether it's defensiveness, avoidance, or overcompensation—and question where they stem from.

A useful exercise is to ask: When faced with stress or uncertainty, how do I instinctively react? Do I withdraw, become aggressive, or seek control? Once a leader identifies their conditioned response, they can begin to disrupt the pattern by choosing a different course of action.

Intentional Change: Rewiring Leadership Behaviors

Breaking free from conditioned patterns is not about erasing the past but about transforming it into wisdom. Intentional change requires deliberate effort and consistent practice. Neuroscience has shown that the brain's plasticity allows for new neural pathways to form when old habits are replaced with conscious choices.

One way to initiate change is through "pattern interruption"— deliberately responding differently in situations where an automatic reaction would typically take over. If a leader tends to react defensively to criticism, they can practice pausing, breathing, and responding with curiosity instead of defensiveness. Over time, this new behavior becomes a habit.

Additionally, leaders must redefine their narratives. Instead of saying, I have always been this way, they can shift to I am actively evolving. This mindset fosters growth and allows for continuous self-improvement.

Leadership is not just about guiding others—it is also about mastering oneself. Conditioned patterns can be powerful barriers to growth, but with self-awareness, intentional effort, and the courage to confront internal limitations, leaders can break free. By doing so, they not only enhance their own effectiveness but also create environments where innovation, trust, and collaboration thrive. True leadership is not about being bound by the past but about shaping a future that reflects one's highest potential.

Crafting Your Leadership Identity.

Once you've uncovered your blueprint and broken free from limiting patterns, the next step is to intentionally craft your leadership identity. This is a process of defining who you want to be as a leader and ensuring that your actions, decisions, and interactions align with that vision. Leadership is not merely about authority; it is about influence, authenticity, and the ability to inspire and guide others toward a shared goal. Crafting your leadership identity requires introspection, continuous learning, and the courage to lead with conviction.

Defining Your Leadership Vision

Your leadership identity begins with a clear vision. Who do you aspire to be as a leader? What values do you want to embody? Your vision should serve as a guiding principle in your daily actions and long-term goals. Take time to reflect on the qualities of leaders you admire and analyze what makes them effective. Identify which of these qualities resonate with your own values and aspirations. Crafting a personal leadership statement can help solidify your vision. For example, you might say, "I am a leader who fosters innovation, encourages collaboration, and leads with integrity."

Aligning Actions with Values

Once you have defined your leadership vision, the next step is ensuring that your actions align with your values. Authentic leadership is about consistency; people trust leaders who practice what they preach. This means making decisions that reflect your core principles, even when faced with challenges or pressures. If honesty is a key component of your leadership identity, then transparency in communication should be a priority. If empowerment is a value you hold, then creating opportunities for your team's growth should be embedded in your leadership approach.

Developing Emotional Intelligence

An essential part of crafting your leadership identity is developing emotional intelligence (EQ). A great leader understands their own emotions and those of others. This involves self-awareness, self-regulation, motivation, empathy, and social skills. Practicing active listening, being open to feedback, and managing stress effectively are all ways to enhance EQ. Leaders who demonstrate emotional intelligence build stronger relationships and foster a more engaged and productive team.

Leading with Authenticity and Adaptability

Authentic leadership requires embracing your unique strengths while also recognizing areas for growth. Trying to mimic another leader's style without incorporating your own personality and values can lead to inconsistency and a lack of credibility. Instead, embrace what makes you unique and refine your leadership style based on real-world experiences. At the same time, adaptability is crucial. The challenges you face as a leader will evolve, and so must your approach. Being open to learning, adjusting strategies, and responding to new situations with agility is key to long-term leadership success.

Building a Legacy Through Leadership

Finally, crafting your leadership identity is about leaving a lasting impact. Leadership is not just about personal success—it is about shaping the success of others and the organization as a whole. Consider the legacy you want to leave. Do you want to be remembered as a leader who inspired, innovated, or uplifted others? Taking intentional steps to mentor, empower, and create meaningful change will ensure that your leadership identity stands the test of time.

By defining your leadership vision, aligning your actions with your values, developing emotional intelligence, leading with authenticity, and focusing on your legacy, you can craft a leadership identity that is both powerful and enduring. Leadership is a journey, not a destination, and the effort you put into shaping your identity today will determine the impact you create tomorrow.

Passing Down the DNA: Legacy and Influence.

True leadership extends beyond the confines of a tenure or job title; it is about the impact that resonates through generations. A leader's true measure is not solely in the achievements attained during their time but in the values, vision, and influence they impart to others. Passing down leadership DNA ensures continuity, fostering a culture of resilience, purpose, and transformation that shapes individuals long after the leader has moved on.

Leadership DNA consists of a leader's principles, ethics, and mindset—the foundational traits that define their approach to challenges, decision-making, and interpersonal relationships. Unlike positional authority, which fades with time, leadership DNA is a living legacy that can be instilled in teams, mentees, and organizations. It is a transfer of not just knowledge, but wisdom; not just strategies, but ideologies.

One of the key elements of passing down leadership DNA is mentorship. A true leader invests in the growth and development of others, recognizing that their success is amplified when others thrive. Through mentorship, guidance, and coaching, leaders impart their experiences, lessons, and vision to those who will carry the torch forward. Whether through structured mentorship programs or informal coaching moments, the investment in people ensures that the leader's influence persists even in their absence.

Another vital component is fostering a strong organizational culture. Culture is the invisible thread that binds a group together, shaping behaviors, expectations, and aspirations. Leaders who actively build a culture of integrity, accountability, and innovation leave an indelible mark on their teams. They set a standard of excellence that continues to guide decisions and actions long after they have departed. By embedding their values into the fabric of the organization, they create a sustainable environment where their leadership DNA thrives.

Leadership DNA is also transmitted through storytelling and lived experiences. The most effective leaders understand the power of narratives in shaping beliefs and inspiring action. By sharing their journey, struggles, and triumphs, they provide a roadmap for others to follow. These stories become guiding beacons, offering lessons that transcend time and circumstance. A compelling leadership story does not just recount success; it reveals vulnerability, resilience, and the unwavering commitment to a greater cause.

Moreover, leadership is about empowerment—giving others the confidence and tools to lead in their own right. True leaders do not hoard knowledge or authority; they distribute it. By encouraging autonomy, critical thinking, and problem-solving, they cultivate leaders rather than followers. This empowerment fosters a legacy of self-sufficiency and innovation, ensuring that their influence is not limited to replication but evolution.

Ultimately, passing down leadership DNA is about building something greater than oneself. It is about crafting a legacy that is not confined to personal achievements but is woven into the fabric of those who have been inspired, guided, and transformed. The greatest leaders are not remembered solely for what they did but for what they enabled others to do. Their impact is not measured in accolades but in the continued growth of those who carry forward their principles, ensuring that leadership is not just a moment but a movement that transcends time.

Building your Leadership DNA is a lifelong journey of self-discovery, growth, and impact. It requires unearthing your unique blueprint, breaking free from limiting patterns, and intentionally crafting the leader you want to be. Ultimately, leadership is not about perfection but authenticity. It's about leading in a way that aligns with your core values and empowers others to do the same.

Through this journey, you don't just lead—you inspire. And in doing so, you leave a legacy that transcends.

CHAPTER 6

REDEFINING SUCCESS IN LEADERSHIP

In a world obsessed with results, leadership often falls into the trap of being solely about outputs—profits, accolades, metrics, and the quantifiable measures of success. But this vision of leadership is incomplete. Leaders who solely chase these external markers can lose sight of the deeper purpose of their roles and may find themselves leading with a sense of emptiness, disconnected from their teams and their own sense of fulfillment. They may even burn out in the process, feeling that the climb to the top has become a race with no finish line.

True leadership is not just about what's achieved but how it is achieved. It's about the people you lead, the culture you build, and the long-term legacy you leave behind. It's about creating value that transcends the immediate bottom line and fosters an environment where others can grow, thrive, and make their own contributions to the larger mission. Leadership is about guiding others to reach their potential and helping them realize their own sense of purpose.

A leader who is only focused on short-term wins may overlook the most important aspect of leadership: building trust. Trust is the foundation of any meaningful relationship, and the leader's ability to foster it within their team is essential. Leaders who focus only on results often fail to engage with their team on a human level. They may be quick to issue commands but slow to listen, to empathize, or to offer support when it's needed. This can lead to disengagement, resentment, and ultimately, decreased performance.

True success in leadership lies in the creation of a culture where individuals feel valued, seen, and heard. It's about building relationships based on mutual respect and understanding, where people know that their contributions matter and that their well-being is prioritized. When leaders take the time to nurture these relationships, the results they achieve are more meaningful and sustainable because they are rooted in trust, respect, and collaboration. Leaders who focus on their team's growth, development, and empowerment create a ripple effect that goes far beyond any single project or initiative. These leaders understand that their impact is measured not just by what they accomplish in the moment but by the long-lasting effect they have on others.

This shift from a results-driven approach to a purpose-driven one doesn't mean abandoning the importance of results altogether. It means reimagining what success looks like. Instead of measuring leadership solely by the numbers—whether it's sales figures, profit margins, or productivity—leaders should also evaluate their effectiveness by how well they are fostering a healthy, thriving, and engaged team. A successful leader is one who brings out the best in others, not just one who hits targets.

In addition to relationships, true success in leadership is also about upholding values. Leaders who prioritize integrity, authenticity, and empathy are more likely to create environments where others feel safe to take risks, share ideas, and pursue their passions. Values provide the compass that guides decision-making, especially during times of uncertainty or crisis. When a leader stays true to their values, they create an environment where others can align with a shared sense of purpose, which in turn fosters a strong, cohesive team.

One of the greatest misconceptions about leadership success is that it's a destination—something that can be achieved and then left behind. In reality, leadership is a journey, one that requires constant reflection, adaptation, and growth. A leader who redefines success understands that their journey is about more than just the destination—it's about the ongoing process of learning, evolving, and growing alongside their team. This type of leadership is grounded in humility, recognizing that true success is not about being perfect but about being present, engaged, and open to learning from both successes and failures.

Ultimately, success in leadership should be measured by the impact you have on others and the legacy you leave. It's about creating a ripple effect that extends far beyond the immediate organization or project, affecting lives in a meaningful and lasting way. Leaders who embrace this broader vision of success can cultivate environments where both individuals and teams can flourish—not just in the short term, but for the long haul. When leaders prioritize people, relationships, and values, they redefine success in a way that inspires sustainable growth, authentic connection, and a deeper sense of fulfillment.

The Problem with Traditional Leadership Success

Traditional leadership success is often framed in terms of goals achieved: revenue targets met, projects completed, or promotions earned. While these benchmarks are important, they don't tell the full story. A leader might achieve impressive results while leaving a trail of disengaged employees, ethical compromises, or personal exhaustion in their wake.

This approach to success is inherently flawed because it:

Ignores the Process: Focusing solely on results neglects how those results were achieved. Were employees supported or overworked? Was the process ethical? Did it align with the leader's values?

Prioritizes Quantity over Quality: In the rush to hit targets, leaders may sacrifice long-term sustainability for short-term gains.

Leaves Leaders Feeling Empty: Achieving goals without alignment to purpose often leaves leaders wondering, *Is this all there is?*

To redefine success, leaders must broaden their perspective and embrace a more holistic approach.

Take the story of Alex, a CEO of a fast-growing tech startup. By traditional standards, Alex was a massive success—he scaled the company from a small team to a multimillion-dollar enterprise in just five years. But beneath the surface, Alex felt miserable.

He was working 80-hour weeks, constantly stressed, and disconnected from his family. His team, while productive, was burned out and disengaged. One day, after missing his daughter's school recital, Alex had an epiphany. He realized that his version of success wasn't working for him or his team.

Alex decided to step back, delegating more responsibilities to his leadership team and implementing policies to improve work-life balance. Though the company's growth slowed slightly, morale improved, and Alex found fulfillment in leading a company that prioritized people over profits.

Redefining Success: A Holistic Approach

Redefining success in leadership requires shifting the focus from "what" you achieve to "how" and "why" you achieve it. This involves considering factors such as:

Impact on People: Are you creating an environment where people thrive?

Alignment with Values: Are your decisions consistent with your personal and organizational values?

Sustainability: Are your results built to last, or are they short-lived?

Personal Fulfillment: Do you feel purpose and satisfaction in your leadership journey?

With these guiding principles in mind, let's explore the subtopics that delve deeper into what redefining success in leadership truly means.

Beyond Titles and Trophies: What truly defines a successful leader.

In the corporate world, leadership success is often measured by titles, revenue growth, or industry accolades. While these metrics signify achievement, they fail to capture the essence of leadership—its impact on people. True leadership is not defined by hierarchical positions or financial outcomes but by the strength of relationships built along the way. A successful leader fosters trust, inspires teams, and creates an environment where individuals can thrive.

The Power of Trust-Based Relationships

At the heart of impactful leadership lies trust. A leader who cultivates genuine relationships with their team fosters a culture of transparency, accountability, and mutual respect. Employees who trust their leaders are more engaged, productive, and willing to go the extra mile. They don't simply follow orders—they align with a shared vision. Without trust, even the most strategic plans and ambitious goals crumble under the weight of skepticism and disengagement.

Trust is built through consistency, integrity, and empathy. Leaders who listen actively, acknowledge mistakes, and support their teams during challenges cultivate an environment where employees feel valued. A workforce that believes in its leadership is more resilient in times of uncertainty and change, making trust an essential currency of long-term success.

Empowering Others: The True Legacy of Leadership

Successful leadership is not about personal accolades; it's about elevating others. The most influential leaders recognize that their success is measured by the growth and achievements of those they lead. When leaders prioritize mentorship and development, they create a ripple effect—empowering individuals to reach their full potential, take ownership of their roles, and become leaders themselves.

This shift in focus from self to others fosters a culture of collaboration rather than competition. Instead of hoarding knowledge and authority, great leaders share opportunities, provide constructive feedback, and celebrate collective victories. They recognize that leadership is not about control but about enabling others to succeed.

Emotional Intelligence: A Leader's Greatest Asset

Technical expertise and strategic thinking are valuable, but they pale in comparison to emotional intelligence (EQ). Leaders with high EQ understand their own emotions and those of their team members, allowing them to navigate conflicts, inspire motivation, and foster psychological safety.

A leader who exhibits self-awareness and emotional regulation sets the tone for a healthy work environment. When employees feel heard and understood, their morale and commitment increase. Leaders who acknowledge struggles, offer support, and show vulnerability when appropriate build deeper, more meaningful connections with their teams.

Long-Term Success Over Short-Term Wins

While financial performance and efficiency matter, they are short-term indicators of success. Sustainable leadership is about shaping a legacy that outlasts one's tenure. Leaders who invest in relationships create organizations that withstand adversity, adapt to change, and continue to thrive long after they have moved on.

In the end, leadership is not about titles or trophies; it's about the people whose lives are transformed by your influence. The most successful leaders are not those who command the loudest but those who listen the most, not those who take credit but those who give it, and not those who seek power but those who empower others.

Take Emma for example - a call center manager, inherited a team with high turnover and low morale. Instead of focusing on immediate performance metrics, Emma prioritized building relationships with her employees. She implemented open-door policies, weekly one-on-ones, and small gestures of appreciation.

The result? Employee satisfaction skyrocketed, and so did productivity. Emma's focus on relationships proved that investing in people leads to sustainable success.

Key Lessons

- Relationships are the foundation of effective leadership.
- Trust and empathy are more valuable than technical skills.
- Focusing on people leads to better results in the long run.

Values Over Victories: Leading with Integrity.

True leadership is not measured solely by victories, profits, or accolades but by the unwavering commitment to integrity.

Success built on compromises and shortcuts may offer immediate gains, but it is often short-lived and unsustainable. Leaders who prioritize integrity ensure their actions align with their core values, even when doing so is inconvenient or costly. This principle defines authentic leadership and establishes a foundation of trust, respect, and long-term success.

Integrity in leadership means making decisions that reflect honesty, fairness, and ethical responsibility. It requires leaders to uphold principles even when faced with difficult choices. In today's competitive world, the pressure to deliver quick results can tempt individuals to cut corners, manipulate data, or overlook ethical concerns. However, true success does not come from momentary wins achieved at the expense of values; it comes from fostering a culture of transparency and accountability. A leader who prioritizes integrity builds credibility and earns the trust of employees, stakeholders, and customers. Trust, once established, is invaluable and strengthens an organization's reputation and stability.

One of the key challenges of leading with integrity is navigating situations where ethical decisions come at a personal or professional cost. A leader may face resistance, financial setbacks, or even backlash for standing by their principles. Yet, the long-term benefits outweigh the short-term sacrifices. When employees witness leadership grounded in ethical decision-making, they are more likely to embody those values in their work. This creates a culture where honesty and responsibility are the norm rather than exceptions. Organizations with strong ethical foundations often experience greater employee engagement, reduced turnover, and enhanced productivity because their workforce believes in the mission and leadership.

History offers countless examples of leaders who chose values over victories and, in doing so, left lasting legacies. Figures like Mahatma Gandhi, Nelson Mandela, and Martin Luther King Jr. championed justice and integrity, even in the face of immense opposition. In the corporate world, leaders like Satya Nadella of Microsoft have demonstrated how ethical leadership fosters innovation, inclusivity, and long-term success. These individuals proved that prioritizing values does not mean forsaking success; rather, it strengthens it.

Conversely, numerous cases highlight the downfall of leaders who prioritized short-term victories over integrity. Scandals like Enron and Volkswagen's emissions fraud demonstrate how unethical decisions may yield temporary success but ultimately lead to reputational ruin, legal consequences, and the erosion of stakeholder trust. These cautionary tales underscore the importance of aligning actions with ethical standards, regardless of external pressures.

Ultimately, leadership is not just about winning but about winning the right way. Leaders who operate with integrity inspire others, create meaningful impact, and build legacies that endure beyond their tenure. In a world where success is often measured by profits and power, the most valuable currency remains character. By prioritizing values over victories, leaders not only achieve genuine success but also contribute to a better, more ethical world.

When a major client asked Sarah, the CEO of a sustainable fashion brand, to cut corners on environmental standards, she refused—even though it meant losing a lucrative deal. Her decision reinforced her company's commitment to sustainability and earned her team's respect.

Key Lessons

- Integrity builds trust and long-term success.

- Compromising values for short-term gains undermines credibility.

- Leadership is about doing what's right, not what's easy.

Sustaining the Journey: Avoiding Burnout and Building Resilience.

Leadership is a marathon, not a sprint. The journey of leadership requires endurance, adaptability, and resilience.

Those who seek long-term success must develop strategies to sustain their energy and effectiveness while fostering a culture of resilience within their teams. Avoiding burnout and maintaining resilience is not just about self-care; it is about fostering an environment where individuals can thrive, innovate, and contribute effectively over time.

Understanding Burnout in Leadership

Burnout is a state of emotional, mental, and physical exhaustion caused by prolonged stress and overexertion. Leaders often face immense pressure to meet expectations, drive results, and support their teams, which can lead to burnout if not properly managed. The symptoms of burnout include chronic fatigue, reduced performance, detachment, and a diminished sense of accomplishment. If left unaddressed, burnout can impact decision-making, productivity, and overall workplace morale.

Strategies to Avoid Burnout

Prioritize Self-Care - Leaders must recognize that their well-being directly influences their ability to lead effectively. Regular exercise, proper nutrition, and adequate sleep are essential to maintaining high energy levels. Additionally, incorporating mindfulness techniques, such as meditation or deep breathing exercises, can help manage stress and enhance focus.

Set Realistic Goals and Boundaries - Many leaders fall into the trap of overcommitting and setting unrealistic expectations for themselves and their teams. Establishing clear boundaries between work and personal life is crucial. Learning to delegate responsibilities and trusting team members to handle tasks reduces unnecessary pressure and fosters a collaborative environment.

Develop a Support System - Leadership can often feel isolating, but having a strong support network can make a significant difference. Seeking mentorship, engaging in peer discussions, or joining professional networks can provide valuable perspectives and guidance. Encouraging open conversations about challenges and stressors also helps normalize the need for support.

Encourage Work-Life Balance Within the Team - Resilient teams are built on the foundation of work-life balance. Encouraging employees to take breaks, use their vacation time, and disconnect from work outside office hours contributes to a healthier and more productive workforce. Leaders should model this behavior to reinforce its importance.

Emphasize Purpose and Motivation - A clear sense of purpose fuels resilience. Leaders should regularly remind themselves and their teams of the "why" behind their work. Connecting daily tasks to a greater mission enhances motivation and prevents feelings of monotony and burnout.

Building Resilience for Long-Term Success

Resilience is the ability to recover from setbacks, adapt to challenges, and keep moving forward. Developing resilience involves cultivating a growth mindset, embracing challenges as learning opportunities, and maintaining a positive outlook. Encouraging a culture of continuous learning, celebrating small wins, and providing constructive feedback all contribute to long-term success.

Leaders who sustain their journey through resilience and energy create a lasting impact. By prioritizing well-being, fostering support systems, and promoting a balanced work culture, they ensure their teams remain engaged and motivated. True leadership is not just about reaching goals but about sustaining the drive to inspire and lead others for the long haul.

Purpose Beyond Profit: Measuring Impact That Matters

In today's world, businesses and leaders are increasingly recognizing that true success is not solely measured by financial gain but by the impact they create in people's lives and the broader society. Profitability remains a key indicator of a company's viability, yet sustainable and meaningful success is rooted in purpose—an aspiration to create lasting, positive change. Leaders who embrace this perspective shift from a purely transactional mindset to one that prioritizes transformation, ensuring that their organizations contribute meaningfully to communities, employees, and global well-being.

A purpose-driven approach requires leaders to redefine success in a way that extends beyond quarterly earnings reports. Instead of solely maximizing shareholder value, they should focus on delivering stakeholder value—an inclusive framework that considers employees, customers, communities, and the environment. Companies that successfully integrate purpose into their business models foster greater customer loyalty, employee engagement, and long-term sustainability. Studies have shown that businesses committed to social responsibility tend to outperform their competitors, demonstrating that impact and profit are not mutually exclusive.

One of the most compelling examples of measuring impact beyond profit can be seen in companies that prioritize sustainability and ethical business practices. Organizations that invest in renewable energy, fair wages, and community development create a ripple effect that benefits society at large. Patagonia, for instance, has built a brand identity around environmental activism, committing a percentage of profits to ecological conservation. This commitment not only strengthens its corporate identity but also deepens its relationship with consumers who share similar values.

Similarly, in the aviation and service industries, companies that prioritize customer experience and employee well-being often see increased operational efficiency and profitability. In a wheelchair service operation, for instance, focusing on the well-being of disabled passengers by ensuring adequate staffing, training employees in compassionate care, and leveraging data analytics to optimize services leads to a better passenger experience. While these efforts may not immediately translate into higher profit margins, they generate long-term goodwill, brand loyalty, and ultimately, sustainable revenue growth.

Leaders who measure success through impact must establish clear and actionable metrics. Traditional financial indicators such as revenue and profit margins should be complemented by social and environmental impact measurements, including employee satisfaction, customer well-being, carbon footprint reduction, and contributions to local communities. For instance, companies that actively track their diversity, equity, and inclusion efforts and set benchmarks for improvement demonstrate a commitment to positive societal change.

Furthermore, innovation plays a crucial role in driving purpose-driven success. Companies that embrace technological advancements to solve pressing societal challenges often find themselves at the forefront of their industries. Whether through artificial intelligence optimizing healthcare accessibility or data-driven solutions enhancing aviation services, integrating innovation with purpose creates meaningful change while maintaining financial sustainability.

Ultimately, success should be viewed as the legacy leaders leave behind. It is about shaping organizations that inspire, uplift, and improve lives, rather than simply generating revenue. By redefining success beyond profit and embedding impact-driven strategies into their core operations, businesses and leaders contribute to a more sustainable and equitable world—one where true success is measured by the difference they make.

Redefining success in leadership is not about abandoning results—it's about achieving them in a way that aligns with your values, supports your team, and creates lasting impact. By focusing on relationships, integrity, sustainability, and purpose, leaders can build legacies that go beyond metrics and accolades.

True leadership success is about more than what you achieve; it's about how you achieve it and the lives you touch along the way.

The Visionary Within

Leadership, at its core, is about envisioning possibilities that others cannot yet see. It is about inspiring people to believe in a future that is brighter, better, and more meaningful. But vision isn't just about the external—the grand plans, the strategies, and the milestones. The most profound visions often emerge from within, rooted in a deep understanding of who you are, what you value, and why you lead.

The problem is that many leaders focus outward, trying to conform to external expectations or mimic the success of others. They look for blueprints instead of trusting their inner compass. But the truth is, you cannot inspire others to follow a vision if you haven't cultivated the visionary within yourself.

This chapter is an exploration of how to discover and harness the visionary within. It challenges conventional notions of vision as something grand and external, reframing it as a deeply personal and internal process. Through this lens, we'll uncover what it means to be a visionary leader in today's complex, rapidly changing world.

Vision: More Than a Buzzword

In the world of leadership, "vision" is one of the most overused and misunderstood terms. We often think of visionaries as larger-than-life figures—Steve Jobs revolutionizing technology, Elon Musk dreaming of life on Mars, or Martin Luther King Jr. inspiring a generation to fight for civil rights. While these examples are inspiring, they can also feel unattainable.

The truth is, visionary leadership isn't about being extraordinary; it's about being authentic. A visionary leader isn't someone who predicts the future but someone who creates it by aligning their values, passions, and actions with a meaningful purpose.

True vision begins within. It's about understanding what drives you, what challenges you, and what legacy you want to leave behind. It's about tapping into your unique perspective and daring to think differently.

The Blind Spots of Visionary Leadership

Being a visionary leader isn't always glamorous. While the ability to see beyond the present and chart a new course for the future is often celebrated, the journey is fraught with challenges that can make leadership isolating and demanding.

Visionaries are often met with skepticism, resistance, and self-doubt, all of which can impede progress if not carefully managed.

Facing Skepticism and Resistance

One of the biggest hurdles visionary leaders encounter is skepticism from others. Bold ideas that challenge the status quo can be met with doubt, not because they lack merit, but because they disrupt established norms and require people to step outside their comfort zones. Employees, stakeholders, or even the public may resist change, fearing uncertainty or potential failure. This resistance can create significant friction, slowing down the implementation of new initiatives or leading to outright rejection of ideas that could be transformative.

Furthermore, organizations often operate within rigid structures and bureaucracies that can make it difficult for visionaries to gain the necessary support. Many leaders find themselves in a constant battle to justify their ideas, defend their decisions, and convince others of their feasibility. In some cases, the most groundbreaking ideas only gain acceptance after initial failures or after someone else successfully implements a similar vision.

The Weight of Self-Doubt

Even the most confident visionary leaders are not immune to self-doubt. The burden of pushing forward a vision that others may not yet understand can be overwhelming. There are moments when setbacks and criticism make even the strongest leaders question their direction. They may wonder if they are too idealistic, if their goals are unattainable, or if they have the resilience to continue in the face of adversity.

This internal struggle can lead to hesitation, causing leaders to second-guess their decisions or water down their ideas to gain broader acceptance. When self-doubt creeps in, it can hinder creativity and boldness, diluting the very essence of what makes visionary leadership powerful.

The Risk of Burnout and Isolation

The relentless pursuit of a vision can take a toll on a leader's mental, emotional, and even physical well-being. Visionary leaders often work long hours, continuously strategizing and problem-solving, leaving little time for personal rest and reflection. The expectation to consistently inspire and motivate others can be exhausting, especially when facing significant obstacles.

Additionally, the visionary path can be isolating. Many leaders find themselves feeling alone, as their perspective and aspirations are not always shared by those around them. Colleagues and peers may not fully grasp the depth of their vision, leading to a sense of detachment. This isolation can further compound stress and exhaustion, making it harder for leaders to stay the course.

Navigating the Challenges

To overcome these blind spots, visionary leaders must cultivate resilience, patience, and adaptability. Building a strong support network, fostering open communication, and embracing collaboration can help mitigate feelings of isolation and self-doubt. Additionally, taking time for self-care and reflection is crucial to maintaining long-term effectiveness.

While being a visionary leader comes with its challenges, those who persist through the skepticism, resistance, and personal struggles often leave a lasting impact. Their ability to see what others cannot—and to bring that vision to life despite adversity—defines true leadership.

The Journey to Uncovering Your Inner Visionary

Unlocking your visionary potential starts with introspection. It requires asking yourself questions like:

- What do I deeply care about?

- What impact do I want to create in the world?

- What fears or insecurities are holding me back?

These questions are not always easy to answer. They require honesty, vulnerability, and a willingness to confront uncomfortable truths. But the rewards are worth it. By connecting with your inner visionary, you gain clarity, confidence, and a renewed sense of purpose.

Maria was a high school teacher who felt unfulfilled despite a decade of success in her career. She loved teaching but sensed that her impact was limited to the walls of her classroom. After much reflection, Maria realized her true passion was improving education access for underserved communities.

With no prior experience in leadership, Maria launched a nonprofit to provide scholarships and mentorship programs for disadvantaged students. Her vision was met with skepticism, but Maria's unwavering belief in her mission inspired others to join her cause. Today, her organization has changed the lives of thousands of students, proving that ordinary people can become extraordinary leaders when they tap into their inner vision.

Key Principles of Visionary Leadership

Authenticity Over Imitation: Don't try to replicate someone else's vision. Your unique perspective is your greatest strength.

Clarity and Communication: A vision is only as powerful as your ability to communicate it. Make it simple, relatable, and inspiring.

Adaptability: Visionaries must balance conviction with flexibility, knowing when to stay the course and when to pivot.

Courage to Dream Big: Great visions often feel impossible at first. Embrace the discomfort of thinking beyond what's safe or familiar.

Dream Big, Start Small – The Blueprint for Building Vision

Visionary leaders often grapple with the challenge of translating big dreams into tangible actions. The gap between an ambitious vision and its execution can seem daunting, leaving many overwhelmed or stuck in perpetual planning. However, the key to success lies in a balanced approach—dreaming big while starting small. By anchoring a grand vision in concrete, achievable steps, leaders can create a sustainable path toward realization.

Defining the Vision

A compelling vision is the foundation of any successful endeavor. It provides direction, inspires action, and aligns efforts toward a common goal. However, crafting a powerful vision requires clarity and purpose. Leaders must ask themselves: What change do I want to see? What impact do I aim to create? A well-defined vision should be aspirational yet attainable, motivating yet realistic.

Equally important is the ability to communicate this vision effectively. A leader must articulate their dream in a way that resonates with stakeholders—whether employees, investors, or communities. The vision should evoke passion and commitment, turning abstract ideas into a shared purpose that drives collective action.

Breaking Down the Vision into Actionable Steps

Once a vision is established, the challenge shifts to execution. The key to making progress lies in breaking down the vision into small, manageable steps. This approach prevents overwhelm and provides a roadmap for continuous movement toward the ultimate goal.

Set Micro-Goals: Instead of attempting to achieve everything at once, divide the vision into short-term objectives. These should be specific, measurable, attainable, relevant, and time-bound (SMART). Each micro-goal serves as a milestone, keeping momentum alive.

Prioritize and Sequence Tasks: Not all actions need to happen simultaneously. Leaders should identify the most critical tasks and tackle them first. By sequencing efforts effectively, they can maximize impact and avoid resource burnout.

Leverage Small Wins: Achieving early success, no matter how small, builds confidence and motivation. Celebrating progress reinforces commitment and demonstrates that the vision is not just a distant dream but an unfolding reality.

Adapting and Iterating Along the Way

The journey from vision to execution is rarely linear. Unexpected challenges, shifting priorities, and external factors often require adjustments. Agile leaders embrace flexibility, allowing room for iteration and improvement.

Gather Feedback: Engaging stakeholders in the process fosters alignment and collaboration. Regular feedback ensures that the vision remains relevant and adaptable to changing circumstances.

Refine the Strategy: As leaders progress, they should reassess strategies and make necessary course corrections. This iterative process ensures continuous improvement and increases the likelihood of long-term success.

Sustain the Vision: Maintaining enthusiasm for a long-term vision requires persistence. Leaders should consistently reinforce the purpose behind their efforts, keeping themselves and their teams inspired despite obstacles.

Dreaming big is essential for transformational leadership, but without action, visions remain mere aspirations. By starting small and implementing structured, incremental steps, leaders can turn ambitious ideas into reality. A clear vision, coupled with disciplined execution, creates a roadmap for sustained progress, proving that even the grandest dreams are built one small step at a time.

Overcoming Self-Doubt – The Inner Critic vs. the Inner Visionary.

Self-doubt is one of the most formidable barriers to effective leadership. Even the most successful leaders experience moments of hesitation, questioning their abilities, decisions, and impact. However, what separates visionary leaders from those who stagnate is their ability to silence their inner critic and amplify their inner visionary. Understanding this dynamic and learning how to navigate it is crucial for unlocking one's full leadership potential.

The Inner Critic: The Voice of Doubt and Fear

The inner critic is that persistent voice in our minds that magnifies our failures, minimizes our achievements, and instills fear of inadequacy. It often manifests as imposter syndrome, perfectionism, or excessive caution, leading to paralysis and hesitation in decision-making. This internal voice stems from past experiences, societal expectations, and deep-seated fears of failure or rejection. If left unchecked, the inner critic can lead to self-sabotage, reduced confidence, and an aversion to taking necessary risks.

Leaders who succumb to their inner critic may find themselves second-guessing decisions, struggling with delegation, or avoiding difficult conversations. This self-doubt can create a ripple effect, causing uncertainty among their teams and hindering organizational progress. The key to overcoming this barrier is not to eliminate the inner critic entirely but to recognize and reframe its influence.

The Inner Visionary: The Voice of Confidence and Purpose

Contrasting the inner critic, the inner visionary is the voice of clarity, confidence, and purpose. It is the guiding force that enables leaders to see beyond obstacles, envision possibilities, and inspire those around them. The inner visionary is not about arrogance or blind optimism but about trusting oneself, learning from failures, and maintaining resilience in the face of challenges.

Cultivating the inner visionary requires intentional effort. Leaders must engage in self-reflection, identify their core values, and develop a clear sense of purpose. Visionary leaders understand that failure is not a definitive measure of their worth but rather a stepping stone for growth. They acknowledge their limitations but do not allow them to define their potential.

Strategies to Silence the Inner Critic and Amplify the Inner Visionary

Reframe Negative Self-Talk — Instead of allowing the inner critic to dominate, challenge its assertions. When self-doubt arises, question its validity and replace negative thoughts with constructive affirmations. Instead of thinking, "I'm not good enough," shift the mindset to, "I am continually learning and improving."

Seek Constructive Feedback — Leaders often assume they must have all the answers. However, seeking feedback from mentors, peers, and team members can provide valuable perspective and validate strengths that self-doubt obscures.

Take Action Despite Fear – Courage is not the absence of fear but the willingness to act despite it. Visionary leaders make decisions based on principles rather than fear-driven hesitations. Each step taken in alignment with a clear vision strengthens confidence.

Embrace Failure as Growth – Every successful leader has faced failure. The difference lies in how they interpret it. Instead of seeing failure as a reflection of incompetence, view it as a necessary experience for growth and innovation.

Develop a Support System – Surrounding oneself with positive influences, mentors, and like-minded individuals can help counteract self-doubt. External support provides encouragement and guidance when the inner critic grows too loud.

Self-doubt is an inevitable part of leadership, but it does not have to be a limiting force. By recognizing the inner critic's voice and choosing to amplify the inner visionary, leaders can cultivate resilience, clarity, and confidence. The most impactful leaders are not those who never doubt themselves, but those who refuse to let doubt define their journey. When the inner visionary takes precedence, leadership transforms from hesitant to transformative, guiding both the individual and their organization toward success.

Turning Ideas into Impact – From Concept to Execution.

A vision is only as powerful as its execution. Many brilliant ideas remain unrealized due to a lack of clear strategy, proper planning, and effective execution. Transforming ideas into impactful outcomes requires a structured approach that bridges the gap between conception and realization. This section provides a roadmap for systematically developing and implementing ideas to create meaningful change.

Every impactful idea starts with a clear vision. A well-defined vision provides direction, motivation, and purpose. When articulating a vision, it is essential to answer key questions:

- What problem does the idea solve?
- Who benefits from its execution?
- What does success look like?
- What resources are required to bring the idea to life?

Clarity in vision ensures alignment among stakeholders and sets the stage for structured execution.

Developing a Strategic Plan

Once a vision is established, the next step is to create a roadmap to execution. This involves:

Setting SMART Goals: Objectives should be Specific, Measurable, Achievable, Relevant, and Time-bound.

Identifying Key Stakeholders: Understanding who needs to be involved, from team members to investors, is crucial.

Assessing Risks and Challenges: Recognizing potential obstacles and developing contingency plans helps mitigate setbacks.

Allocating Resources: Budget, personnel, technology, and materials should be accounted for to ensure smooth implementation.

A well-structured plan transforms an abstract idea into a concrete action framework.

Building the Right Team

Execution requires collaboration. A strong team with diverse skills is essential for turning ideas into reality. Consider:

Assigning Roles and Responsibilities: Clearly defined roles ensure accountability.

Encouraging Innovation and Ownership: Team members should feel empowered to contribute their expertise and take initiative.

Fostering Communication and Transparency: Open dialogue ensures alignment, addresses concerns, and keeps progress on track.

Executing with Agility

Execution is rarely linear; it demands flexibility and adaptability. Key elements of effective execution include:

Breaking the Plan into Phases: Implementing the idea in stages allows for better management and monitoring.

Using Project Management Tools: Platforms like Trello, Asana, or Microsoft Project streamline workflows and enhance efficiency.

Gathering Continuous Feedback: Regular check-ins, performance metrics, and stakeholder insights help refine execution strategies.

Measuring Impact and Adjusting Strategies

Success is determined by measurable impact. Evaluating outcomes ensures that the vision is effectively realized. Key performance indicators (KPIs) should be established to assess:

Effectiveness: Did the idea achieve its intended purpose?

Efficiency: Were resources used optimally?

Scalability: Can the idea be expanded for greater impact?

Regular assessments allow for necessary adjustments and improvements.

Sustaining and Scaling the Impact

Ideas should not just be executed; they should be nurtured for long-term sustainability. Strategies to ensure lasting impact include:

Documenting Best Practices: Learning from successes and failures aids future projects.

Developing a Support System: Mentorship, partnerships, and stakeholder engagement sustain progress.

Iterating and Innovating: Continuous improvement ensures relevance and scalability.

Turning ideas into impact requires more than inspiration; it demands strategic execution. By defining a vision, developing a plan, assembling the right team, executing with agility, measuring results, and ensuring sustainability, ideas can evolve into powerful, transformative realities. A great idea alone is not enough—it is execution that ultimately makes the difference.

Inspiring Others – How to Share and Sustain Your Vision.

A vision is more than just a dream or a statement of intent; it is the driving force behind leadership, innovation, and collective success. However, a vision that is not effectively communicated or shared with others remains an isolated idea with limited impact. The true power of a vision lies in its ability to inspire others, mobilizing them toward a common goal. To achieve this, leaders must not only articulate their vision clearly but also cultivate an environment where it is sustained and reinforced over time.

Communicating a Vision That Resonates

Clarity and Simplicity: A compelling vision should be clear, concise, and easy to understand. Complexity can lead to confusion, diminishing the enthusiasm of those who might otherwise support it. When a vision is straightforward, people can easily relate to it and see where they fit within it.

Emotional Connection: People are not just driven by logic; they are motivated by emotion. A strong vision taps into emotions by painting a picture of a better future and the role each person plays in achieving it. Storytelling is a powerful tool in this regard, as it makes the vision personal and relatable.

Authenticity and Passion: A leader who genuinely believes in their vision can ignite passion in others. Authenticity breeds trust, and when people trust the leader's sincerity, they are more likely to commit to the vision. Passion is contagious—when leaders demonstrate their unwavering belief, it motivates others to invest their energy as well.

Inclusivity and Engagement: A vision should not be imposed; it should be shared and co-created with others. Engaging stakeholders—employees, partners, and even customers—in the process fosters ownership and commitment. Encouraging input and collaboration helps ensure that the vision is embraced by those who will bring it to life.

Sustaining the Vision Over Time

Leading by Example: Actions speak louder than words. Leaders must embody the vision in their daily decisions, behaviors, and interactions. When people see that the leader consistently upholds the values and principles of the vision, they are more likely to follow suit.

Consistent Communication: Reinforcement is key to sustaining a vision. Regularly communicating progress, celebrating small wins, and reminding people of the bigger picture keeps the vision alive. Meetings, newsletters, storytelling sessions, and company-wide updates can all serve as tools for reinforcement.

Aligning Systems and Structures: A vision cannot thrive in an environment where policies, structures, and incentives do not support it. Organizations must align their operations, training, and reward systems with the vision to ensure that people have the resources and motivation to work toward it.

Empowering Others: Leaders should cultivate other champions of the vision. By mentoring and developing future leaders who share the same passion, the vision becomes self-sustaining. Encouraging initiative and providing autonomy enables people to take ownership and drive the vision forward.

Adaptability and Resilience: A vision should be dynamic, not static. The world is constantly evolving, and a rigid vision may become obsolete. Leaders must be willing to adapt their vision in response to new challenges while staying true to its core purpose. By remaining resilient and flexible, the vision can withstand setbacks and continue to inspire.

Sharing and sustaining a vision requires more than just stating it; it involves active engagement, authenticity, and continuous reinforcement. When leaders communicate with clarity, inspire through passion, and align systems to support their vision, they create an environment where people are not just followers but active contributors. A truly inspiring vision does not fade—it evolves, strengthens, and endures through the collective commitment of those who believe in it.

The visionary within you is your most powerful leadership tool. By embracing authenticity, overcoming doubt, and translating dreams into action, you can inspire meaningful change. Leadership isn't about having all the answers—it's about daring to ask, "What if?" and having the courage to find out.

The End

Leadership is not a title, a position, or even a destination—it is a journey. It is the act of continuously discovering who you are, how you show up in the world, and what you leave behind for others. This book has explored the layers of leadership, delving deep into the human experiences that shape, challenge, and ultimately reveal the leader within each of us.

From the mirror that leadership holds up to our innermost selves, to the scars of broken hearts and shattered self-esteem, we've seen how personal history and emotions influence the way we lead. We've explored the delicate balance between competence and complaints, the fine line between aggression and assertiveness, and the unrelenting weight of "not being enough." At each turn, we've uncovered the truth that leadership doesn't create something new in us—it simply magnifies what has always been there.

True leadership begins with awareness. It's about facing the uncomfortable truths that lie within and understanding how they shape our decisions, behaviors, and relationships. A leader who has faced their fears, embraced their imperfections, and leaned into their vulnerability becomes someone who leads not from fear or ego but from courage and authenticity.

Yet awareness alone is not enough. Leadership demands action. It requires the courage to dream big but with the wisdom to start small. It asks us to turn ideas into impact, to overcome self-doubt, and to build a vision that inspires others. Leadership is as much about the choices we make in quiet moments as it is about the decisions that shape the course of history.

The stories shared throughout this book remind us that leadership is deeply human. From the teacher-turned-changemaker to the coffee shop entrepreneur and the artist who almost quit, these real-life examples illustrate that leadership is not reserved for the extraordinary. It is accessible to anyone willing to step up, take responsibility, and create a meaningful impact.

Above all, leadership is about relationships. A leader cannot exist in isolation; they are defined by the people they serve, inspire, and collaborate with. Visionary leaders know how to connect deeply, communicate authentically, and foster environments where others can thrive. They understand that leadership is not about control but about influence—not about being the loudest voice in the room but about creating a space where every voice matters.

As we conclude, it's important to recognize that leadership is not static. It evolves as we grow, adapt, and respond to the world around us. Each challenge we face, each lesson we learn, and each success we achieve adds another layer to our leadership DNA.

Leadership is not about perfection; it's about progress. It's about striving to be better—not for recognition, but because the world needs better leaders. It's about leaving behind a legacy not of power or fame but of lives touched, minds inspired, and hearts transformed.

The question is not whether you have what it takes to be a leader. The question is: Are you willing to embark on the journey of becoming? The visionary within you is waiting. It's time to step forward and lead.

.

ABOUT THE AUTHOR

Fouad Kanneh is an emerging aviation professional, accountant, data analyst and website application developer.

Before joining the United States aviation industry, Fouad spent over a decade promoting the values of the United Nations and principles of generation equality and global citizenship, in the West Africa region. He also led several projects for the United Nations system in Sierra Leone.

As an international public speaker, Fouad has engaged several international decision-making platforms including the United Nations Headquarters in New York, USA.

www.ingramcontent.com/pod-product-compliance
Lightning Source LLC
LaVergne TN
LVHW042109190726

843493LV00006B/1414